TALES FROM THE
SAN FRANCISCO 49ERS
SIDELINE

A COLLECTION OF THE GREATEST
49ERS STORIES EVER TOLD

ROGER CRAIG
WITH MATT MAIOCCO
AND DANIEL BROWN

FOREWORD BY
BILL WALSH

SPORTS
PUBLISHING

Sports Publishing books may be purchased in bulk at special discounts for sales promotion, corporate gifts, fund-raising, or educational purposes. Special editions can also be created to specifications. For details, contact the Special Sales Department, Sports Publishing, 307 West 36th Street, 11th Floor, New York, NY 10018 or sportspubbooks@skyhorsepublishing.com.

Sports Publishing® is a registered trademark of Skyhorse Publishing, Inc.®, a Delaware corporation.

Visit our website at www.sportspubbooks.com.

10 9 8 7 6 5 4 3 2 1

Library of Congress Cataloging-in-Publication Data is available on file.

ISBN: 978-1-61321-228-8

Printed in the United States of America

This book is dedicated to my wife, Vernessia, who has been by my side through all the ups and downs of my career. She always supported me, giving me comfort in bad times and keeping me level headed when things were going great.

— R.C.

CONTENTS

FOREWORD

My relationship with Roger Craig has developed over a period of many years after scouting him, drafting him and coaching him with the 49ers. Our rapport has continued to grow in recent years, too. Roger has so many fantastic qualities to like and respect. He is a very genial, open and communicative person, and he is somebody you can trust.

The things we have been through together with the 49ers enabled us to tear down any boundaries that sometimes separate coaches from players. All of this started when we drafted Roger from the University of Nebraska in 1983.

His college career was remarkable because of his willingness to sacrifice for his team. He accepted his role as primary blocker for Mike Rozier, when in reality Roger was superior to Rozier in every respect. But Rozier could not play fullback, so Roger filled that job.

That kind of unselfishness sent him back to the second round in the draft. We were very fortunate to acquire him. The minute you saw Roger on the field, you could tell he had unique athleticism. Roger had the quickness and speed, the explosiveness and agility, the leaping ability and acceleration anybody would want out of a running back. He immediately became a mainstay of our offense.

For a period of time, Roger played fullback for us. But in our offense, the fullback and halfback positions were comparable. With Wendell Tyler and Roger, we had one of the best backfields the game has ever seen. Later, when Roger moved to halfback, he teamed with fullback Tom Rathman to provide another of the great backfields in the history of the game. Roger simply did everything we asked of him during his time with the organization.

Roger's work ethic was stellar. And his outstanding abilities, combined with his hard work, took him far. A lot of players were just as determined to work hard as Roger, but they simply could not keep up with him. His physical regimen was unbelievable. Roger Craig and Jerry Rice were probably two of the most driven and best conditioned athletes to play the game.

As one of the team's unquestioned leaders, Roger brought along the whole squad. He was in that mold from the minute he came to the 49ers. He won just about every physical skill and fitness award that we handed out.

The year that we were lucky enough to draft Roger, he was exactly what we were looking for. I could not have projected that he would play as well as he did, just like I couldn't make that kind of prediction on Jerry Rice. I knew both of those players would be good, but you're never sure if they'll end up being great.

But as soon as Roger took the practice field, you could tell that we were talking about a special athlete. He ran with those high knees, making him beautiful to watch and difficult to tackle.

Roger had outstanding speed and elusiveness and great hands as a receiver. When we had workouts with him, he caught everything thrown his way, so we knew his receiving skills weren't going to be a problem. But NFL personnel people questioned his hands because they had no clue. None of them had ever seen him catch a pass in a game.

Of course, we asked our backs to catch, block and run. During that time, a lot of NFL offenses didn't have the kind of dimensions that we insisted upon at the 49ers.

There was a period of time when Roger was easily one of the best three or four running backs in all of football. I remember John Madden stating flat out that Roger was the best back in the league. I heard that quite a few times in the mid- to late 1980s.

In another offense, Roger would easily have gained a lot more yards rushing. But we combined rushing and pass receiving. We looked at total yards, not just rushing yards from our backs.

He had an outstanding career, with the highlight perhaps coming in Super Bowl XIX when he scored three touchdowns against the Miami Dolphins. He continued on to be one of the great running backs in NFL history. He is a clear-cut Hall of Famer, and some day he will be honored as such.

Even when our team was not at its best, Roger was still there leading his teammates. In those days, a 10-6 record was considered a bit of a disappointment for us. Roger always stepped up in the toughest games and the fiercest weather conditions to handle the ball and provide a spark to ignite the team.

I'm not sure the days of the 49ers in the 1980s will ever be duplicated because of the circumstances in the NFL today. We had many great athletes on one team. Yet we had competition that you couldn't believe. The Giants and Redskins had their own dynasties. It was an era of truly great teams in the NFC. We'd have to meet each other along the way just to get to the Super Bowl. And in those important games, Roger was always at his best.

Even to this day, whatever challenges and responsibilities he faces in work and in life, he tackles with the same energy, enthusiasm and insatiably positive attitude. He is a wonderful family man with a beautiful wife and children and he has done extremely well for himself since leaving football.

Roger and I are like son and father—or, I'd prefer to say, brothers. It's a very, very close relationship. He is a true representative of the game of football and of the San Francisco 49ers during that magical time in the franchise's history.

BILL WALSH

ACKNOWLEDGMENTS

I'd like to recognize my five children for working for everything they have achieved and never expecting anything to be given to them just because they have a "celebrity dad." Vernessia and I could not be any more grateful for our three daughters, Damesha, Rometra and Nia-Jai, and our two sons, Rogdrick and Alexander. We are extremely proud parents.

Thanks to my mother, Ernestine, for her unwavering support through my life. Also, I want to express my gratitude to my brother, Curtis, for setting a high standard on and off the playing field for me to follow and try to surpass.

There isn't a day that goes by that I don't think of three influential family members who are no longer with us. My father, Elijah Craig, always told me, "Be the best you can be," and I've tried to live by those words. My oldest sister, Brenda Martinez, was an inspiration to me. My aunt, Cordelia Moore, was my biggest fan and always cheered the loudest at my games.

I was lucky enough to have some coaches who presented me with the foundation on which to build my career. My junior high coach, Lou Williams, was an inspiration and a motivational figure in my life. Jim Fox, my high school coach, was also a tremendous teacher. My running backs coach at Nebraska, Mike Corgan, taught me mental toughness.

A special thanks to Vivek Ranadive, a close friend and the chairman and CEO at TIBCO Software, Inc. Vivek, who is known as "the father of real-time computing," is the Bill Walsh of the software world. His product is the West Coast Offense of software. The system is flexible and dependable—all in real time.

Thanks to my many teammates, coaches and everyone associated with the 49ers through the years. The meaning of "team" was never lost on us during our many seasons of excellence. And I owe a special debt of gratitude to the 49ers faithful—the fans who supported me when I played and still come up to me just to say "Hi" after so many years.

ROGER CRAIG

My wife, Sarah, did a fantastic job of spending extra hours looking after our little girl, Jane, while I was sequestered in my office working on this book. I love you both very much, and it was always a welcome sight any time you came downstairs to check on me.

I want to thank my family for their support through the years: my father, Ernest; mother, Jeanette; brothers Vince and Marty, and their great wives and children. Also, a big hug goes to my mother-in-law, Mary Munson, for everything she has done.

My grandmother, Billie Laughlin, passed away during the writing of this book. I miss her boundless energy and zest for life.

Thanks to Brad Mangin for being a great photographer and an even better friend. His pictures helped bring this book to life. Also, much appreciation goes to David Armosino, an old Corning High chum whose recommendation to Sports Publishing's Bob Snodgrass eventually led to this project.

A special thanks to the many people I've worked with and learned from through the years, especially Mike Wolcott, Roger Weigel and Dan Pambianco, who were instrumental in my fledgling career. Likewise, thanks to the Humboldt State University journalism department. Also, I'd like to recognize the fine folks at *The Press Democrat*, including George Manes, Bill Pinella, Lowell Cohn and Bob Padecky.

Many thanks to the 49ers' public relations department, headed by Kirk Reynolds, for supplying the research materials for this project; and to the 49ers' beat writers, past and present, for helping make 4949 Centennial Boulevard such a fun work atmosphere.

Also, I'd like to tip my cap to the many 49ers players and front office members who have graciously shared their time with me through the years. Of course, thanks to Roger Craig for approaching this book with the same enthusiasm and generosity that typified his Hall of Fame-caliber career.

MATT MAIOCCO

INTRODUCTION

I had just finished my first season covering the 49ers when I began hearing rumblings that one of the most respected players in franchise history was working out in hopes of making a comeback.

It was early in 1996. The 49ers had just suffered a disheartening 27-17 loss to the upstart Green Bay Packers in an NFC divisional playoff game. The 49ers had virtually no running game, forcing quarterback Steve Young to attempt an NFL playoff-record 65 passes. He also led the team in rushing with 77 yards.

It was the story of the season, really. Although the 49ers finished with an 11-5 record, they were one-dimensional on offense.

Derek Loville was the team's leading rusher, and he averaged 3.3 yards a carry. Fullback William Floyd was lost in the middle of the season with a knee injury. Ricky Ervins, Adam Walker, Jamal Willis, Dexter Carter and Anthony Lynn were also given shots at carrying the ball.

About a month after the season, I saw Roger Craig at a Bay Area restaurant having lunch. I quickly drove home to pick up a notepad and tape recorder and went back to the restaurant and waited for him in the parking lot.

After introducing myself as a reporter, I proceeded to ask him if what I was hearing was correct. Was he really serious about making a return to the NFL to play for the 49ers?

Roger confirmed the whispers I had heard from within the organization. The next day the story was picked up by the wire services and ESPN reported it on *SportsCenter*.

I'll admit, at first I was skeptical of Roger's intentions. Not knowing him personally, I initially figured Roger was another self-absorbed athlete who was out to recapture the glory that was missing from his post-football life. Or perhaps, he was just in it for the big paychecks that come along with a spot in the NFL.

But what I discovered was that Roger was talking about returning to play professional football for only one reason: He wanted to help his team.

Make no mistake, Roger might have played a season with the Los Angeles Raiders and two with the Minnesota Vikings to end his career, but his team was always the San Francisco 49ers.

He played his final season with the Vikings in 1993. In August of the following year, Roger reported to the 49ers' summer home in Rocklin, California, to sign a contract with the team.

His playing days were over, but the 49ers agreed to sign Roger to a contract to provide symbolic closure to his career. Now he was officially retiring as a member of the 49ers.

"He was a man who, when he played, was the epitome of the San Francisco 49ers," former owner Eddie DeBartolo said on that day. "He did everything that was asked of him."

That is why two full NFL seasons later, Roger was ready to don 49ers colors once again. But the only reason he was willing to return to the rigors of the NFL was because he thought he could help a team looking for a running back to replace Ricky Watters, who had left following the 49ers' Super Bowl season of 1994.

Replace Ricky Watters with Roger Craig? What a great idea.

Roger's idea was to sign a contract for the NFL minimum and practice twice a day in the searing heat of Rocklin, and if the 49ers thought he could help the team, fine. If they thought he could not contribute, he would return to his successful life outside of football.

Most veteran players would do anything possible to avoid going to training camp. Roger was eager for the opportunity to return for the unglamorous part of playing in the NFL.

"Let me prove myself, and may the best man win," said Roger, who made a career out of proving himself and re-proving himself during his eight seasons with the 49ers. "I can still catch the ball and do everything the same. I'm available when they call."

Roger watched the 49ers every week during that 1995 season. It was clear to him that the offense was lacking a running back who could get down the field and catch passes to take the pressure off Jerry Rice.

"That's what they need," Roger said in the restaurant parking lot. "When Ricky Watters played, they were zoning him, and that opened up the offense."

No running back in league history had forced defenses to respect his pass-catching skills like Roger, who felt healthy and explosive after two years of avoiding the week-to-week punishment of playing in the NFL.

That call never came.

Maybe he could have helped the 49ers in 1996. We will never know. The 49ers decided to move in another direction. They traded for Terry Kirby in the off season, but that never really solved their problems, either. The 49ers' next reliable back arrived the following year when Garrison Hearst signed as a free agent.

Roger Craig was the ultimate team player during his seasons with the 49ers. Even in retirement he had the organization's best interests at heart.

That is why when I had the opportunity to work on a book about the 49ers, it was only natural that Roger Craig should be the individual to have his stories chronicled.

After all, Roger Craig is the epitome of the 49ers.

MATT MAIOCCO

Chapter 1

THE
PROTOTYPE

When I was coming into the NFL in 1983, the running back position was a lot different from today. Back then, if you were a running back, you ran the ball. That was pretty much all that was asked of you. My versatility was never really put to the test at the University of Nebraska, where we churned out yards on the ground with the help of some of the biggest and most talented offensive lines in college football.

But with Coach Bill Walsh, an offensive mastermind who was acquiring the pieces for his puzzle, the San Francisco 49ers were changing the way football was to be played.

And clearly, this was not just a fad around the NFL.

The running back had to do a little bit of everything in Coach Walsh's revolutionary system. I am very proud of my role in helping to shape the way the game is now played, with the added emphasis on running backs who can catch the ball out of the backfield.

Look around the NFL today and you'll see every team using elements of the West Coast Offense. Look around the NFL today and you'll see running backs doing what I helped make popular back in the 1980s.

I take a lot of pride in leading the way for the great running backs of today—players such as Marshall Faulk, Edgerrin James, Priest Holmes, LaDainian Tomlinson, Deuce McAllister and Tiki Barber. Not only are those players among the league leaders in rushing, they also amass a large number of pass receptions and are invaluable members of their respective offenses.

Coach Walsh has called me the "prototype" running back for his system. Of course, I had the physical gifts, but it also took a lot of hard work to get to the point where Coach Walsh and the 49ers could depend on me year in and year out.

After having an up-and-down college career, during which only a small percentage of my talents were displayed, I knew I was going to have to earn everything on my own at the next level. But until I went to the 49ers and to Coach Walsh, I had no idea what the level of my true potential was.

Disappointing Senior Year

After rushing for 1,060 yards in my junior season at Nebraska, I had high hopes—and Heisman hopes—as a senior. But I was unable to fulfill those dreams because I moved to fullback to begin my senior season. In Nebraska's offense, the fullback did not have nearly the diversified role as the position I would play with the 49ers. My job was primarily to block for Mike Rozier, with whom I shared time as the featured back the previous season.

Early in my senior year, I sustained an ankle injury, forcing me to miss three games. I did not get my starting job back when I was healthy enough to get back onto the field. Later in the season, Mike got injured in a game at Hawaii and I stepped into my familiar role as the featured halfback. Hawaii was beating us

16-0 to start the second half. I ended up carrying 18 times for 127 yards and a touchdown, and we came back to pull out the big road victory.

Our next game was a few weeks later when we played in the Orange Bowl against LSU. Mike was healthy again, and Coach Tom Osborne decided to play him at halfback. I was disappointed, but I also figured that the campaign for Mike to win the Heisman Trophy the following season had already begun. In fact, he did win the Heisman in 1983. He went on to make two Pro Bowls and rushed for 4,400 yards in eight NFL seasons with Houston and Atlanta.

I was disappointed that I did not have the kind of senior year I had envisioned, but with that one game against Hawaii, I showed a glimpse of what I could do. I began to focus on impressing the NFL scouts.

I was invited to play in the Hula Bowl and the Senior Bowl. I went to the Hula Bowl and played well enough that I did not need to go to the Senior Bowl and risk another injury before the NFL draft in April of 1983.

Preparing to Join 49ers

With my primary job as a blocker in the Nebraska offense, I rushed for only 586 yards as a senior. Instead, I had to make my mark with a couple good workouts at the NFL scouting combines.

I saw some publications that would rank the top running backs, and I was generally No. 3 behind Eric Dickerson and Curt Warner. I continued to work out and run and catch some passes so I'd be ready for the draft.

About three weeks prior the draft, I read in *Sports Illustrated* that the 49ers thought I was the prototype for the kind of back they wanted—a player who was big, strong, fast and willing to block.

"Wow, the 49ers are interested," I thought. "Maybe I should start catching more passes."

I caught only 16 passes in four seasons at Nebraska, but I knew the 49ers liked to throw passes to their running backs. During my daily workouts, I'd catch at least 100 passes a day. Basically, I was preparing to become a member of the San Francisco 49ers.

On draft day, Dickerson and Warner went with the second and third overall picks to the Los Angeles Rams and Seattle Seahawks, respectively. I was hoping to be selected shortly after them, but luckily I had to wait for several more hours.

Waiting for my name to be called was agonizing, but eventually I would be satisfied with what fate had dealt me. Still, it was difficult to see other running backs being drafted ahead of me. Philadelphia selected Michael Haddix at No. 8; Detroit took James Jones five spots later; then Gary Anderson went to San Diego with the 20th overall pick.

The 49ers did not have a pick in the first round. There weren't any other running backs taken for a while. But before the 49th pick of the draft, which coincidentally happened to belong to the 49ers, the phone rang.

Coach Bill Walsh was on the line. He asked if I wanted to be a 49er. I said, "Hell, yeah!"

Perfect Fit

The 49ers were the perfect team for me. They really did not have any standout running backs in 1982, so I knew there were no superstars like Walter Payton against whom I had to compete for playing time. I had to report to training camp prepared to make an immediate contribution.

The year the 49ers won the Super Bowl in 1981, Ricky Patton was the leading rusher with 543 yards. The next season, when they played just nine games because of the strike, Jeff Moore led the team with 281 yards. Earl Cooper might have been their best back, but he was still trying to get comfortable at one position because he had been used at both fullback and tight end.

There was going to be an opportunity for me to play immediately, but I knew I had to develop my pass-catching skills. After all, the 49ers didn't know if I had good hands because I was never called upon to catch the ball in college.

Developing Into My Role

Around the time of the draft, the 49ers acquired veteran half-back Wendell Tyler in a trade with the Los Angeles Rams for two draft picks. That meant that I would go to the 49ers as a fullback, and at six feet, 222 pounds, I was ready to do anything Coach Walsh asked of me.

When I reported to training camp with all the other rookies, it was three days before the veterans were scheduled to show up. I wanted to make an impression and feel comfortable before the entire team got there.

Paul Hackett was the 49ers' offensive coordinator and quarterbacks coach, and he taught me the offense. He also got me ready for what I would experience in my role with this team. He threw me hundreds of passes over three days. I dropped three balls the whole time.

Coach Walsh was right there. He saw that I could catch the football. In his offense, he needed a versatile fullback who could catch the ball when something wasn't open down the field. Much of the offense's success in the early 1980s was built around the fullback.

And all those passes I caught in my workouts after my senior year at Nebraska paid off. My rookie season with the 49ers, I was the team's second leading receiver with 48 catches—three times more passes than I caught in four years at Nebraska.

Voluminous Playbook

I was blown away when I caught my first glimpse of the 49ers' playbook. At Nebraska, where we had a lot more running plays than passing plays, we really did not have much to learn.

But with the 49ers, it was like I had just completed my work at a university and began pursuing a postgraduate degree in the NFL. Everything with the 49ers was so detail oriented that you really had to pay attention during classroom time. After all, one misstep could destroy the whole play.

I quickly realized that the system was so complex, it forced us to study hard and learn all of our responsibilities. But even that wasn't enough. We also had to learn everybody else's responsibilities.

Everybody had to be accountable on every play. If I picked up the wrong guy on a blitz, that could have ended up being the final play of Joe Montana's career.

Our coaches did a great job of getting us to feel comfortable with the offense. Sherm Lewis, our running backs coach at the time, took the time to tutor me and break down the offense. He stressed the fundamentals of the game. We worked on the basic plays and the basic formations before moving onto the more complex plays and formations. He wanted to emphasize the foundation of the entire offense—the passing routes, different holes to run through, and pass protections—before we started to learn the other stuff, which would become the icing on the cake.

Learning the Intricacies

As a rookie with the 49ers, I found myself thinking about small details of the game that I had always taken for granted at the high school and college levels. Quarterback Joe Montana and Wendell Tyler were especially helpful in getting me to recognize the importance of the little things.

After practice, Joe and I would work on little facets of the game that probably get overlooked by today's athletes. We used to spend time working on play-action fakes. Coach Walsh made me understand what I had to do as a player and what my role would be. I knew I wasn't going to carry the ball 30 times a game, so I had to learn to do all the little things.

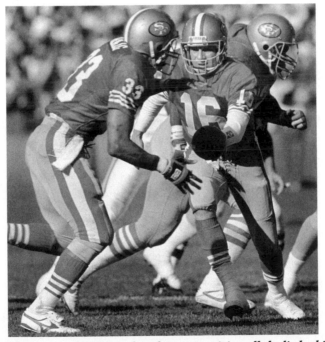

Joe Montana and I spent a lot of time practicing all the little things, such as taking hand offs and play-action fakes. (Photo by Brad Mangin)

Coach Walsh said he brought me to the 49ers for my toughness and attitude. He had a way of getting guys to fit into his mold for the family, and he clearly had a vision of how he would use my skills to complement the rest of the team.

My primary duty was to be a blocker for Wendell, but I think I shocked a lot of people with my versatility. I proved I could block, catch and run. I had to adapt to the new style of offense, so I spent a lot of time working on all the subtleties of the position.

Wendell was a good guy to follow. Being a veteran running back, he held my hand a little and led by example. I learned a lot from him, especially looking at the way he practiced and how he hit the holes. Because he was coming from the Rams, he was also learning a new system, so we were able to help each other.

Comparisons Made

It was always uplifting when the coach would say something positive about your abilities. Early in my first training camp, Coach Walsh saw something he liked in the way I approached my job.

"He is just what the doctor ordered," Walsh told newspaper reporters less than two weeks into my first training camp. "He has great stamina and hasn't missed a step."

Apparently, when the 49ers drafted me they likened my style to Freeman McNeil, the Pro Bowl running back with the New York Jets. But Walsh amended his comparison after watching me up close for a week or so of training camp.

"I think he's closer to Franco Harris as a runner," Walsh said. "He's a Franco type of player. He could be as good a blocking prospect who plays the position. He gets to people in a hurry and takes them down."

Not-So-Grand Beginning

I battled injuries throughout my senior year at Nebraska, and my rookie season with the 49ers began on an ominous note.

In the first preseason game of 1983, Raiders defensive end Lyle Alzado slammed me down on a play and I landed on the ball. I sustained torn cartilage in my rib cage, and I could not practice because the pain was so severe.

One night during training camp, I was watching one of the Sacramento television stations in my dorm room in Rocklin, California, where we held training camp. The sportscaster started dogging me because of my injury. He said, "The 49ers' first pick is already hurt, and it looks like he's going to be a bust."

It pissed me off. I missed two preseason games, but I was determined to play in the final tune-up against the Seattle Seahawks. I knew I had to show everybody what I could do and that I was not going to be a bust.

We got beat 20-6 at Candlestick Park, but Coach Walsh didn't seem to mind because his squad was taking shape for the regular season. I remember him telling the team in the locker room afterward, "We might have gotten beat, but we found out we got us a runner in Roger Craig. Give him a hand."

Determined to Practice

After that first training camp, in which I missed practice time due to my rib injury, I was determined in future years not to spend any time on the sideline.

Coach Walsh would give out awards on the night before we broke training camp. He would give an award to anyone who made it through the entire camp without missing any practices.

Although I didn't win it my rookie year, I made a habit out of getting on the practice field for the rest of my career. I won that award seven years in a row, picking up a television set or a dinner jacket as the prize on a yearly basis.

People took pride in winning that award, and it certainly meant a lot to me. I knew the more guys who were able to make it all the way through camp without taking time off, the bigger edge we would have as a team during the season.

A Back for All Downs

One of the big keys to the West Coast system is having a running back who never has to leave the field.

In the early 1980s, every team had a third-down specialist who would come into the game and be used as a pass receiver. It became predictable for defenses, because they knew that the offense was going to throw the ball.

But if you had a prototype running back for this West Coast system who never had to leave the field, it would keep the defenses from catching up. With our system, the defense never knew if we were going to throw the ball on third down or run a draw play.

Because our running backs could stay on the field for third down, our offense was more potent. Wendell Tyler did not have to come off the field on third down. And later, when we got Tom Rathman, I made sure he was ready for the job requirements. After practices, I would throw him pass after pass after pass. If you wanted to play in this offense, you had to catch the football.

Following My Brother

My brother, Curtis, was a great player, and I learned the importance of establishing a strong work ethic from him. He is five years older than me, so I always looked up to him. And I'm in total agreement with my high school coach, Jim Fox, that I could not have gone wrong by following the example of my older brother.

"The way I look at it, Curtis was the perfect role model for Roger," Jim Fox said. "Curtis was the essence of everything good. He was a great kid and he was hard-working. Roger was lucky to have such a great role model."

Curtis was a wingback at Nebraska and quite the local celebrity in Davenport, Iowa, where we grew up. He was the guy I tried emulate. In fact, I aspired to be better than my brother because he set the bar so high.

As a junior at Central High School, I broke my right leg, so it was important to have someone pushing me during my rehabilitation. Before my senior year of high school, I worked out regularly with my brother. Years later, I would take it upon myself to help set the tempo in practice for those great 49ers teams by pushing my teammates to work harder.

When I first came to the 49ers, I would sprint 50 to 70 yards down the field on every play. The veterans did not know how to take that, but it soon became contagious. Now it is a way of life with the 49ers and a lot of other teams in the NFL.

I'm not sure the veterans knew how to take me at first, but it didn't take too long for everyone else to start catching on. When Jerry Rice came to the 49ers in the 1985 draft, he knew what he had to do. He had to follow my lead because now everybody practiced that way. Jerry is now known for his tremendous work ethic, but when he came into the NFL, he was just trying to keep up with the guys who had already been around for a while.

That is the way 49ers practices have continued since the day I left the organization. Even though Coach Steve Mariucci came to the 49ers seven years after my days with the 49ers were finished, I'm told that he continued to demand that players practice that way. It's nice to see that my legacy continued on the 49ers' practice field.

Hurdler at Heart

The most distinguishing feature of my running style was the way I got my knees up when I ran. I didn't learn how to run that way in the pros or even in college. I first developed that form as a sixth-grader and refined it while running the high hurdles.

I used to love to watch my brother, Curtis, during his two-a-day summer practices at Central High. I vividly recall watching the players run through drills and hearing running backs coach Jack Leabo screaming at them: "Get your knees up!"

Because I knew there would be a day when I would play football for Coach Leabo and head coach Jim Fox, I figured I better start making it a habit to run with high knees before I even got to high school. After all, I didn't want anyone yelling at me for making mistakes.

My running style enabled me to break simple arm tackles at every level. In one high school game, I inadvertently knocked out three defensive players when my knees hit them under the chinstrap. Instead of absorbing the big hits, I was administering them as a running back.

I was, and still am, a track-and-field fanatic. My football running style helped me when I was running the hurdles—and my form in the high hurdles helped me on the football field, too.

Ira Dunsworth, my track coach, taught me the correct form to use on the track. I finished in second place in the 110-meter

high hurdles and the 400 hurdles at the Iowa State Track and
Field Championships my senior year. I found that I could be
even more effective on the football field if I applied the same
principles of running with my knees up.

Meeting "Skeets"

I always followed track and field, and I'm still a big fan of the
sport. After running the hurdles in high school, I also ran the
indoor track season my junior year at Nebraska, placing fourth
in the 60-meter high hurdles at the Big Eight championships.
The sport is definitely in my blood.

So when the 49ers drafted me, I was in awe of one player in
particular who would become my teammate. It wasn't Joe
Montana or Ronnie Lott. The man I looked forward to meeting
the most was someone who had not even made his name as a
football player.

I thought, "Wow, I'm going to be teammates with Renaldo
Nehemiah." I could not wait to meet him. He was the best hur-
dler of his generation, and he signed with the 49ers in 1982
after Coach Walsh figured his athleticism would enable him to
be a dangerous wide receiver in the NFL.

Renaldo and I worked out together and talked a lot about
track. Nobody knew how to approach him because he was a
track guy. Track was my first love, so we were able to connect.
We remain pretty good friends to this day.

Party Off

I knew this was going to be a serious job during my first training camp with the team in Rocklin.

I went up to Ronnie Lott early during camp and asked him where I could find a party that night. We had a day off the next day, so I was looking to enjoy myself a little.

Well, Ronnie looked at me with that angry look, his eyebrows furrowed, and said, "We didn't draft you to come here and party. We drafted you to help us get back to the Super Bowl. Instead of partying, you should study your playbook."

That stunned me. But I knew right then these guys meant business. That was the first week of training camp, and I decided it was best to remain well rested and use that evening, as well as my day off, to study the playbook.

After that, I was always trying to validate myself to the veterans who had worked so hard to be professionals. I wanted to prove to the team that I had the work ethic it took to succeed and I wasn't just some snot-nosed rookie who came into camp thinking he was hot shit.

Party On

I now knew that a training camp in Rocklin was no party. I never went out searching for a good time again, but one night toward the end of my first training camp, the party found me.

I was always good about deferring to the veterans. I respected those guys because they had been there before me and had already proved themselves at the professional level. I surrounded myself with guys who knew the business and had the savvy to put together long and successful careers—guys such as

Lawrence Pillars, Fred Dean, "Hacksaw" Reynolds, Gary "Big Hands" Johnson, Keith Fahnhorst and John Ayers.

One night some of those guys decided to get a couple of the rookies drunk. Carl Monroe and I were the lucky victims. They made us drink tequila shots all night long, and we staggered out of the bar and back to the dormitories on the Sierra College campus.

I had a hard time getting up in the morning. I had a splitting headache. Some of my teammates would scream in my ear, just to give me the full effects from my first hangover.

Coach Walsh knew what was going on and he didn't seem to mind that much. He just shook his head. He knew the veterans had pulled one over on the naïve rookies.

Hacksaw Endorsement

Jack "Hacksaw" Reynolds was one of the true professionals on those 49ers teams of the early 1980s. He had already had a solid career with the Los Angeles Rams, and he helped bring a winning mentality to the 49ers.

I knew I was doing things right when veteran offensive lineman Keith Fahnhorst came up to me and said, "You're pretty lucky, Roger. Hacksaw doesn't usually give rookies the time of day, so you must be pretty special."

I wanted everyone to know that I wasn't out there to outdo the veterans and showboat. I came to work. Those words—albeit secondhand—from Hacksaw told me that I was on the right path.

No Hazing Zone

The veterans had some fun at the rookies' expense when they took us out for a few drinks, but Coach Walsh did not condone any rookie hazing. He simply did not believe in it—and, boy, was I ever happy about that.

Coach Walsh felt that hazing disrupts the players' concentration and creates a division between the veterans and rookies. After all, the veterans needed the rookies to contribute on the field, yet on some teams the rookies are viewed as second-class citizens.

On other teams, the kids are trying to make the team but they also have to be thinking about giving a speech or putting on a skit or singing a song instead of studying their playbooks. A few years ago, several rookies for the New Orleans Saints got injured when an initiation got completely out of hand.

Coach Walsh was proactive. He knows every year the hazing of rookies gets a little worse than it was the year before. With the 49ers, we were a family, and Coach Walsh tried to foster an attitude that everyone depended on one another and nobody was better than anybody else.

When I went to the Raiders, I joined a team that abused rookies. But when I finished up with the Minnesota Vikings, there was no hazing of rookies. The coach of the Vikings was Dennis Green, and he learned from Bill Walsh.

A Day at Training Camp

The only drawback to being a rookie was you had to show up early in the morning to get your ankles taped because the veterans would have priority the closer it got to practice time.

I'd get up around 7 a.m. and have breakfast before heading into the locker room to get taped for our 8:45 a.m. practices at Sierra College.

The practices in the morning were pretty intense because it was cooler and that was when we did our hitting. Coach Walsh never believed in practicing hard in the afternoon, especially when it was routinely hotter than 100 degrees during training camp.

After a long morning practice, a lot of us would go over to the stands and sign autographs for the fans. Most of the time, there would be 8,000 to 10,000 fans watching us practice in Rocklin. It was great to have that kind of support and to feel the excitement in the stands. Having the fans there kept us motivated to practice hard and do well. The fans were never a pain in the ass. I met families who spent their vacations in Rocklin just to hang out and watch us practice.

We would eat lunch around noon and then go back to our dorm rooms for a little bit of rest. Special teams meetings would begin at 2 p.m., and we were back on the field for a couple hours after those meetings were concluded.

The afternoon practice would end around 5 p.m., which would give us enough time to shower and have dinner and rest a little before the offensive and defensive meetings started at 8 p.m.

The meetings would go until about 10 p.m., and we had an 11 p.m. curfew most of the time. Some nights Coach Walsh would give us a midnight curfew, and some guys would have to go 100 mph just to get back to the dorm on time.

My nickname was Catfish because of the appearance that my eyes were bugging. All I was doing was looking for a place to run. (Photo by Brad Mangin)

Eyes Wide Open

At some point early in my career with the 49ers, receiver Freddie Solomon stuck me with the nickname "Catfish."

It seems like in every picture of me running with the football, my eyes look like they're bugging out of my skull. I never realized I was doing it. Sort of like my high knees, it was just something that happened and I didn't have to think about it.

I think the reason my eyes were always so wide open is because I tried to best utilize my vision to find a hole to run through. Or maybe it was the fear of getting hit. After all, any time you have the ball in your hands, your job is to avoid getting tackled.

Tony Dorsett was the same way. His eyes were always open. I was that way in high school and in college. But people really started noticing it when I was with the 49ers and all those photographers began snapping pictures of me.

Everybody started calling me "Catfish." Heck, even in huddles, Joe Montana would call me "Catfish."

Then Coach Walsh got into the act, too.

Whenever we won, we would watch that game's highlights before our next game. It was Coach Walsh's way of getting us pumped up for the upcoming game. It was also a chance to have some fun.

Before showing the highlights from our previous game, Coach Walsh had an artist paint a picture of a catfish, with exaggerated bubble eyes. Of course, this catfish was wearing a 49ers uniform—No. 33. Everybody got a big laugh out of that when he showed it to the team.

Luckily, I wasn't alone. Joe, who was always being teased about his spindly legs, was being roasted right along with me. Coach Walsh also had a painting done of a stick man wearing No. 16.

I still have that painting of the catfish hanging up after all these years.

Joe Montana and Coach Bill Walsh complemented each other perfectly. Joe could carry out Coach Walsh's instructions exactly as he had drawn them up. (Photo by Brad Mangin)

Reunited on the Field

Just a couple years ago, Steve Sabol, the president of NFL Films, had an idea. He wanted to get Coach Walsh back on the practice field with Joe Montana and some of the other offensive players who helped revolutionize the game.

Joe and I were the only ones who were still in shape. Joe was zipping that ball around like he was still in his prime. I thought that was cool that Steve Sabol would recognize us long after our football careers were over.

I feel good about my role in helping change the game. I was an all-purpose back when there was no such thing.

Now every team strives to have a featured back who can do it all. Players like Marshall Faulk, Edgerrin James and LaDainian Tomlinson are thriving in the NFL today because of their ability to run the football as well as catch it.

I was that kind of running back in the 1980s when there were more pure runners, such as Eric Dickerson, Walter Payton, and later with Barry Sanders. Remember Gerald Riggs of the Atlanta Falcons? All those guys were great runners.

But when I came along, nobody talked about a running back being a threat catching passes. Now it's a big thing, and I'm happy about that. These athletes are evolving and they're getting the most out of their abilities.

Professional scouts now look for backs who can catch the football. With the salary cap, teams can't afford to bring in running backs who are just designated pass catchers.

Chapter 2

COACH WALSH AND THE 49ER WAY

The term "West Coast Offense" started out as an attempt at mocking Coach Bill Walsh's revolutionary system. But just like the offense itself, we managed to turn it around and use it to our advantage.

That is what the "West Coast Offense" is all about.

Through the years, defenses have tried to combat the 49ers-style offense with a variety of schemes. But I remain convinced that with the right players and the right adjustments from the coaching staff, the "West Coast Offense" is just as unstoppable today as it was back in the 1980s when Coach Walsh instituted the system with the 49ers.

Coach Walsh was the 49ers. In many ways, Coach Walsh still is the 49ers. Everything the organization accomplished in the 1980s can be traced back to him. He had the vision and the strength to put his plan into place.

Owner Eddie DeBartolo stepped aside and let Coach Walsh do what he did best—acquire the players to best fit his "West Coast Offense." I just wish Coach Walsh had remained as the coach of the 49ers for a few more years.

Certainly, he was a demanding coach. Through the years, a lot of players could not cope with the commitment Coach Walsh expected from each of his players. He butted heads with some of his players. When compromises could not be reached, those players were often dispatched to other teams in the NFL.

I had a special bond with Coach Walsh. He is the only coach I ever had who knew exactly how to utilize my skills. He knew more about my attributes as a player than I did.

I had nothing bad to say about Coach Walsh when I was playing for him, and I have nothing bad to say about him now. He is the greatest tactician in the history of the National Football League.

What more needs to be said about his ability on the sideline? He inherited a team that went 2-14 in 1978. Three seasons later, he became the first head coach to wear headsets on the sideline—a true indicator of his involvement in the down-to-down strategy of his team.

From 1981 to his retirement after the 1988 season, he won Super Bowls in three of the six non-strike seasons. And with his players and system firmly entrenched, we won another Super Bowl the year after his retirement with George Seifert as coach.

Coach Walsh provided the NFL and the 49ers with a fresh approach. To him, the game of football was a chess match. When we went onto the field, we knew we would always be better prepared than our opponent, and that was half the battle right there.

Thank You, Bengals

Coach Bill Walsh came to the 49ers from Stanford, where he worked wonders with his team in a short period of time. But Walsh would not have been available if it were not for the Cincinnati Bengals' major blunder.

Coach Walsh served on Paul Brown's staff with the Bengals from 1968 to '75. Brown finally decided to step down, and he hand-picked his successor for the 1976 season. He passed over Walsh, who was the team's quarterbacks and receivers coach, and selected offensive line coach Bill Johnson instead.

Johnson did not even make it out of his third season as head coach, while Walsh moved onto Stanford and then to the 49ers in 1979.

Coincidentally, three of Walsh's best victories through the years came against the Bengals. He defeated them twice in Super Bowls, and we also pulled off a miraculous one-point victory with the help of a "Hail Jerry" pass on the final play of a game during the 1987 regular season.

The Boxer

One of the funny things about Brown's decision to pass over Coach Walsh for the head coaching vacancy is that he doubted Walsh was tough enough to wield that kind of power.

This is a guy who fought more than 100 amateur boxing matches, and Paul Brown said Walsh was not tough enough!

I can tell that Walsh was a good boxer, too. We always used to spar together. We would shadowbox before practices. He'd throw a left hook and say, "That one would've gotten you." We had a speed bag at the practice facility, and he would get that thing humming pretty good.

Bill Walsh? Not tough enough? Are you kidding me?

He was definitely tough enough to be a head coach in the NFL. He had to make some difficult decisions during his time running the 49ers, but invariably he seemed to make the right decisions. He would certainly prove that he was smart enough to run an entire franchise. He was the president, general manager and coach.

Owner Eddie DeBartolo demanded everybody perform to the highest possible level, from the coaches on down to the equipment manager. But then he stepped out of it and let Coach Walsh run the show. That's how our dynasty was built. Coach Walsh ran the organization from the marketing down to giving the players contracts.

Coach Walsh commanded respect. I feared him, but I also had—and still have—immeasurable respect for him. He is a special man.

Getting Us Ready

Coach Walsh was a master at motivating his players, and he often used boxing analogies to detail how he wanted us to take apart our opposition.

He would tell us that sometimes the opponent will land a punch here and there and it might make us a little wobbly, but any true champion will keep fighting. The champ is the champ for a reason. He has the experience, and when the other boxer lets his guard down, that's when the champ seizes the opportunity.

To Coach Walsh, the game of football was like a prize fight, but mental preparedness was just as important as physical ability.

The Psychologist

Coach Walsh had a lot of great qualities as a leader. He had an innate knack for knowing how to judge and handle the temperament of his team.

Coach Bill Walsh always had his finger on the pulse of his team. He knew how to deliver the right messages to his players at the right times. (Photo by Brad Mangin)

When we were down, he would find a way to bring us up, and when we were too high on the hog, he knew how to bring us down. He was a mastermind at dealing with people.

He could also keep things light when he felt that was what the team needed. He was always making the guys crack up with different jokes. When he sensed that things were getting tense, that is when he would do something to break the mood.

Before I got to the team, he pulled one of his best stunts during Super Bowl week in January of 1982.

Coach Walsh went to Washington, D.C., to accept a Coach of the Year award the day before the rest of the team left for the Super Bowl in Pontiac, Michigan.

He arrived at the hotel before the team, so he concocted a prank in which he dressed as a bellman and was there to greet the 49ers players. As players stepped off the team bus, Coach Walsh would say, "Let me help you with your bag."

It took a while before the players noticed the bellman was their head coach.

On the day of the 49ers' first Super Bowl, the bus got caught in traffic outside the Silverdome because of then-Vice President George Bush's motorcade. Coach Walsh kept everybody on the bus loose by telling them that the game had already started and the trainer had just thrown a touchdown pass to the equipment manager.

The Fishing Derby

Coach Walsh always knew how to bring a team together. One of the methods he used during training camp was the annual "49ers Fish Derby."

He would set aside one day toward the end of training camp to have a fishing tournament. One of the ponds on campus was stocked with fish. It was a day for the players to bond together and create great camaraderie on the team.

We always looked forward to the fish derby because it was a day to rest our bodies from the rigors of training camp and the team supplied great prizes. The players who caught the biggest fish might get a trip to Hawaii or television sets or some other great prizes. In today's salary-cap era, the NFL probably wouldn't let teams get away with that.

Fans Aplenty

Because of our exciting style of play and all the superstars we had on our teams, we were a big attraction on the road.

We would fly to road games on Friday afternoons and typically get to the team hotel around 11 p.m. or so. Despite the late hour, there would be fans lined up outside waiting to see the "Team of the '80s" get off the bus.

People had a lot of faith in us, and we rarely let them down. I'd always have fans come up to me and say, "You've made me a lot of money. I bet on you guys and you always cover the spread."

It made me want to say, "Well, shit, give me 10 percent."

Making the Tabloids

We had fans all over the world. The 49ers had become not only one of the model franchises in American sports, but were also gaining popularity overseas. Sometimes that meant we found ourselves in the newspapers under stories that caught us completely by surprise.

We opened the 1988 preseason with a game against the Miami Dolphins in London's Wembley Stadium. It was on that trip that I got my first exposure to tabloid journalism. Upon arriving in London, one of the newspapers ran a story entitled, "Roger's 49 Ways to Please His Missus."

Needless to say, the story suggested that my wife, Vernessia, and I did a lot more than just sleep on the flight over the Atlantic. There were even fabricated quotes from my wife in the article.

I didn't give the story much thought after I read it, but unfortunately for me, Joe Montana had brought a copy of the paper onto the plane for the flight home. He made sure everybody on that aircraft saw the story, just in case they missed it the first time.

Vernessia laughed along with the rest of the group, while I just slouched down in my seat and eagerly awaited our arrival back home.

Fielding Requests

Early in my third season, I got called up to Coach Walsh's office.

I still felt like a youngster who was trying to navigate through the NFL, even though my second season ended with a three-touchdown performance in the Super Bowl. I immediately began to wonder if I had done something wrong. I went up to Coach's office, and I was sweating bullets.

"Roger, I like how you're playing," Coach Walsh told me. "We're going to need 100 yards out of you this week."

We were playing the Atlanta Falcons that week. I was the fullback and I wasn't getting a lot of carries, but we knew the Falcons were going to key on Wendell Tyler. I left that office ready to do everything it would take to make sure I cracked 100 yards for my coach. I knew I had to make it happen.

Sure enough, it happened. I broke one run for a 62-yard touchdown. I took the handoff on a quick trap, hit it up inside and then veered toward the left for the touchdown. Afterward I received the game ball for rushing for 107 yards and two touchdowns on just 11 carries.

The Challenge

During the ring ceremony at San Francisco's Palace of Fine Arts after my first Super Bowl, Coach Walsh pulled me aside to talk a little business. He was ready to issue me another challenge.

We were all dressed up in tuxedos for the occasion, which seemed to add something to the moment. Coach Walsh looked me in the eye and told me, "Roger, we're going to need 1,000 yards from you this season."

I was fired up. I knew I couldn't let him down. But then I started to wonder if he meant he needed 1,000 yards rushing or receiving. In 1984, I had 649 yards rushing and 675 receiving.

I wanted to cover my ass, so I figured I better shoot for getting 1,000 yards rushing and receiving.

Making History

It's hard to believe that through the first 61 years of the NFL, nobody had done what I set out to do in 1985.

Coming into the final game of the regular season, I had 978 yards rushing and 960 yards receiving. I knew if I just played my normal game, I would be a charter member of the 1,000 rushing-1,000 receiving club.

But I also had something much more important to accomplish. We needed a victory over the Dallas Cowboys on the final day of the regular season to get into the playoffs.

Late in the third quarter, I caught a 15-yard pass from Joe Montana to achieve the milestone. But my most satisfying moment in the game came when I took a pitch from Joe and carried Dallas linebacker Eugene Lockhart into the end zone for a four-yard scoring run that tied the score at 16-16.

Afterward, I told reporters, "He jumped on my back like a real cowboy."

We went on to a 31-16 victory and a spot in the NFC wild card game, which we lost to the New York Giants 17-3.

Only after the season was I able to reflect and be proud of my accomplishment. I rushed 214 times for 1,050 yards and nine touchdowns, and I caught 92 passes for 1,016 yards and six touchdowns. That season I was named to my first Pro Bowl, and I was a starter in the same backfield as my hero, Chicago's Walter Payton.

Gifts for Linemen

After my 1,000 rushing-1,000 receiving season, I was very grateful for the job of the offensive line. I knew I could not have accomplished this feat without them.

That season, left tackle Bubba Paris, left guard John Ayers, center Fred Quillan, right guard Randy Cross, right tackle Keith Fahnhorst and tight end Russ Francis missed a combined three games. They played together every week, and they built up the continuity it takes for great offensive lines to succeed.

I was extremely grateful for their hard work, knowing full well that I was getting the headlines while they were working their butts off to enable me to get the accolades. I knew I had to do something to show my gratitude.

The older guys—Ayers, Cross and Fahnhorst—loved to go pheasant hunting, so I bought each of the linemen a Browning Citori shotgun with 14-karat gold plating. The inscription read, "Thanks for helping me get 1,000 yards rushing and 1,000 yards receiving."

At the time I paid $1,900 for each of those shotguns. I figure they have to be worth $40,000 or $50,000 now. I've always believed that if your linemen take care of you, you have to take care of your linemen.

Another Great Honor

Probably my most cherished honor that season was being recognized by all my teammates as the winner of the Len Eshmont Award.

Ask any player who has ever suited up for the 49ers, and he'll tell you the Eshmont Award is the most prestigious accomplishment you can achieve. The players vote for the honor, which goes to the person who best exemplifies the inspirational and courageous play of Eshmont.

In 1988, I was again voted as the winner, along with nose tackle Michael Carter. At that point in team history, I joined Paul Hofer, Tommy Hart, Mel Phillips and Jimmy Johnson as the only two-time winners.

West Coast Offense

A lot of people want to know what the West Coast Offense is all about. You can point to the short-passing game that is predicated on rhythm and timing. It can be an offense in which the passes are high percentage and use the same ball-control elements as a running attack.

But to me, the West Coast Offense means no defense can conquer the system.

The system is set up to break any code. There is no defense the system can't break. Whatever a defense wants to try, the West Coast Offense has the answer. I don't believe that will ever change.

The Chicago Bears had their vaunted "46 defense," and everybody tried to find a way to combat it. What the league discovered was that it could be tamed with a short-passing attack. Dan Marino destroyed it with short passes when the Miami Dolphins scored 38 points against the Bears to end their hopes of a perfect season in 1985. He was basically doing it with the West Coast Offense.

The West Coast Offense is an unselfish offense. It doesn't require a running back to carry 25 or 30 times a game. Everybody has to be on the same page, from the offensive line to the quarterback. Everybody has a big responsibility.

Running backs have to be able to pick up blitzes. And we have to be able to do good play-action fakes to bring the safety two or three steps out of his zone. If I do a good play fake and Joe sells it hard, the defense collapses down and Jerry Rice comes across on that slant route.

We understood that as a team. Coach Walsh made us feel every player had a big role on every call. Jerry Rice or John Taylor might get the touchdown, but everybody understood where it all came from. Coach Walsh always said we're all an extension of each other.

Thrilling Win at Cincy

Getting everybody to understand their roles was never more important than in a 1987 game in Cincinnati that forever became known as the "Hail Jerry" game.

We were down 26-20 and the Bengals had the ball on a fourth down with about six seconds remaining. Instead of punting, Cincinnati coach Sam Wyche decided to run one more play in hopes time would expire and the game would be over. But our defense came up with a big play, leaving just two seconds on the clock.

There was time for just one play, so there was no room for error. With our only hope for a victory, Joe Montana lofted a 25-yard pass into the end zone, where Jerry Rice made the leaping catch that enabled us to pull out a 27-26 victory and kept us from dropping to 0-2 on the season.

What I remember about that play is taking care of my job, which was picking up Bengals defensive end Eddie Edwards, who would have gotten to Joe before he could have thrown the pass to Jerry.

This is what our right tackle Keith Fahnhorst said after the game: "I couldn't move to get him or we would have had a holding penalty against us and the play would've been nullified. I just had to leave it up to Rog."

The Thinker

Joe Montana was not the most physically gifted quarterback, but he was smarter than any other quarterback who ever stepped onto the field. He knew how to get rid of that ball on time.

He stuck to the system because he knew the system worked. But he could also improvise as well as any quarterback who ever played the game.

But what made our offense work so well for so long is that he went through his progression of receivers without any hint of panic or urgency. He looked to his primary receiver, and if he was covered, he would go to his secondary receiver. If his second receiver was covered, I was his safety valve.

I was Joe's dump-off guy. I was the guy to whom he could throw the ball in order to keep from getting sacked. I caught 508 passes in my 49ers career, and almost all of them were from Joe.

Joe's cool demeanor enabled him to think clearly and react calmly in any situation throughout his career. (Photo by Brad Mangin)

End Zone Antics

Before Terrell Owens came on the scene, you rarely saw any 49ers players do anything flashy after scoring a touchdown. Coach Walsh certainly would not have stood for it.

I was never one to grandstand or showboat after scoring a touchdown, but there was this one time …

Actually, it still sort of makes me mad when I think back to my second season in the league. We beat the L.A. Rams 33-0. In that game, I caught a swing pass from Joe Montana and took it 64 yards for a touchdown. Upon crossing the goal line, I was so excited that I spun the ball on the end zone grass.

The Rams games were always intense, and any time I scored or did something good, it was extremely gratifying. Those games were like the Nebraska-Oklahoma games.

But my understated celebration apparently broke the NFL rules at the time. The officials penalized me for breaking the new rule against "prolonged, premeditated and excessive celebrations," though I don't think my celebration qualified under any of those descriptions.

Regardless, we were penalized five yards on the ensuing kickoff. Afterward, I told reporters, "I learned from my mistake. I won't do it again." How's that for being diplomatic?

People ask me if I still view the 49ers-Rams rivalry as the same, considering they moved to St. Louis a decade ago. I think the Rams will always be the 49ers' biggest rival. It doesn't matter that they no longer play in Los Angeles. If the Rams played their home games on Mars, it would still be a rivalry.

Jerry Dances

Some time after my "excessive celebration," Jerry Rice began dancing after he scored. His one routine was "The Cabbage Patch," which was a popular dance move in the mid-1980s.

We didn't embrace Jerry's dance too well, but he was in the end zone so often we got to the point where we didn't mind him doing it. He stopped dancing a few years later when he began to view getting into the end zone as part of his job—not some occurrence that was out of the ordinary.

Playing in Pain

Our dedication to the 49ers and to winning football games meant no one ever wanted to come out of the lineup.

In 1986, I played the final 12 games of the season with an injured hip. In the fourth game of the season, I got hit out of bounds against the Miami Dolphins and my left hip came out of the socket.

It was an injury similar to the one that ended Bo Jackson's career. But I played the entire season with the help of cortisone shots, novocaine, and prednisone, a powerful anti-inflammatory. I should have been on prednisone for no longer than 10 days. I ended up taking the stuff for seven or eight weeks.

I still feel the effects from the large doses of prednisone, as the drug ate away at the lining in my stomach and made me anemic. I've experienced ulcers for years and was rushed to the hospital one time that season after the trainers determined that my condition was not just a stomach flu, like they originally believed. Even today, I can't have any dairy products, spicy foods or alcohol because of the damage done to my stomach.

The week after the Miami game, Bill Walsh said he wasn't going to use me unless it was necessary. Late in the first half with us trailing the Indianapolis Colts 14-7, it became necessary.

With Jeff Kemp starting at quarterback in place of Joe Montana, we lined up in the shotgun formation. Center Fred Quillan snapped the ball directly to me, while Kemp was putting on an Academy Award performance, acting as if the ball had sailed over his head. I caught the snap on the run and gained 18 yards through a hole on the right side.

We ended up scoring the tying touchdown on that drive and went on to a 35-14 victory. I finished the game with two rushes for 22 yards.

That game was probably the closest call for me not suiting up. I played the first 128 games of my career until a torn knee ligament in 1990, sustained on the artificial surface at the Astrodome, kept me out of three games.

I suppose I showed the critics who doubted me early on that I could indeed be a durable and reliable running back in the NFL.

No Pain, No Gain

Eric Dickerson wore every pad he could find in order to protect himself from the pounding a running back takes during a game. I was just the opposite. I felt if I wore a bunch of pads, they would just slow me down.

As a result, whenever I played a game, it looked as if I'd spent the afternoon in a cage with a lion.

I did not wear rib protectors or much of anything else. Consequently, I would have welts all over my body from defensive players' facemasks. I was always in a vulnerable position because I caught so many passes out of the backfield, so I was getting blasted from every angle. A lot of times my body was exposed and I didn't have time to protect myself. I was getting hit on just about every play during the course of a game, whether I was running the ball, catching the ball, blocking or carrying out a play-fake.

Running "The Hill"

When I was experiencing the problems with my hip, I discovered it did not hurt as much when I was training if I ran hills.

One day I was running the hills near where I lived when Dr. Arthur Ting, who used to work for the 49ers, saw me. The trail I was running was quite treacherous, and he suggested I try running somewhere that was not quite as potentially hazardous.

He told me to meet him the next day. He showed me another hill and I ran it. I had to stop two or three times to catch my breath, but I made it. Dr. Ting told me, "It will get easier. You just have to fight through it."

I started telling my friends on the team about it. I'd bring them all to the hill—Eric Wright, Keena Turner, Dana McLemore, Mike Wilson, Ronnie Lott and others.

I would even run the hill on my days off during training camp. When we'd have a preseason game, I'd run the hill the next morning before I'd go to Rocklin. I always wanted to feel like I was in control and in good enough shape to conquer anything.

The funny thing is that a lot of people now associate that hill with Jerry Rice. Actually, I'm the one who introduced Jerry to "The Hill". The first time Jerry tried it, he stopped. I had to look for him for two or three weeks to try to convince him to try it again.

But "The Hill" became part of Jerry's training regimen. Without it, he probably wouldn't have lasted in the NFL for as long as he has.

Jerry Rice and I shared a lot of good times on the football field, but it was all work and sweat when we ran "The Hill" together. (Photo by Brad Mangin)

Regaining the Focus

We went 13-2 and won the NFC West during the 1987 season. We had our sights set on a Super Bowl title, but those hopes came crashing down with a first-round playoff loss to the Minnesota Vikings.

It was a devastating loss for us. But the day after the game, Coach Walsh called me into his office to give me news that would force me to get over that loss in a hurry.

I spent my first five seasons in the NFL as a fullback. But Coach Walsh told me he was going to make me the team's half-back in 1988.

Suddenly, I went from being depressed about the loss we had just suffered to being excited about the upcoming season. I wanted to put the team on my back and lead the way to the Super Bowl the following season. I was determined to be in the best shape of my life. I took my family to Hawaii for a vacation, and it was there that I began thinking about what I needed to do to take care of my end of the bargain. Everybody has to be accountable for himself, and I was determined to fulfill all my obligations to Coach Walsh and the 49ers.

I ran "The Hill" even more religiously, and I trimmed down to about three percent body fat. I no longer ate all my favorite late-night snacks, such as raisin-oatmeal cookies with French vanilla ice cream. Instead, I limited my diet to 2,500 calories a day. I was determined to drop 10 or 15 pounds to get my playing weight to about 210.

Three days a week, I'd work on my endurance. Starting at 6:30 a.m., I'd run the four- or eight-mile trails. I'd go up the steep hills at a seven-minute-mile pace, and I'd descend at less than six minutes per mile.

On three other days, I'd do speed work. First I'd do fifteen 100-meter dashes—all uphill. I'd follow that by interval training, running 200-meter sprints with just 30 seconds in between to catch my breath.

Basically, I came into training camp explosive and quick. In other words, I felt like a halfback and not a fullback.

Chiropractice Makes Perfect

My training regimen back in the mid-1980s was controversial because I incorporated a chiropractor into my maintenance program. As *Sports Illustrated* wrote, "Craig may be the only player in the NFL with a private medical staff." I spent $300 a week out of my own pocket on chiropractors and a massage therapist.

In fact, owner Eddie DeBartolo yelled at me over the phone because I was getting therapy that went against the beliefs of the 49ers' medical and training staff. Soon there were 10 or 15 players lined up to get alignments from my chiropractor, Dr. Nick Athens, at our team hotel the night before games. I told Eddie, "If you want to see me on the field on Sundays, then I wouldn't be yelling if I were you."

My mother and grandmother have been going to chiropractors for 35 or 40 years. I was always afraid to get an adjustment. But shortly after my senior year at Nebraska, I met Dr. Mitch Mally during an autograph session at the opening of my cousin's

With all the hits a running back absorbs during the course of a season, it was important to take care of my body and see my chiropractor for regular maintenance. (Photo by Brad Mangin)

gym. I told him I hurt my ankle in an All-Star game. An expert on the lower extremities, Dr. Mally told me he could fix it and have me running faster than ever before in no time. He was right. I saw him two or three times a week the rest of the off season before I reported to training camp. I could feel the changes in my body.

When the 49ers drafted me, I asked him, "Who's going to take care of me in California?" He put me in touch with Dr. Athens, who was practicing the same techniques used by Dr. Mally.

I owe my regular maintenance to the fact I never underwent any major surgery throughout my career. The 49ers team doctors suggested I have surgery on my left shoulder in the 1987 off season, but I declined because I wanted to see if my chiropractor could do anything about it. After a couple visits, my shoulder felt fine. The body is like a car. If you bump into a curb, you don't immediately get a new set of tires; you first get your car realigned. If something is out of line on your body, it sets off a chain reaction from your ankle to your knee to your hip.

It is much more accepted in the NFL today, as many teams have chiropractors on their medical staffs. My advocacy of chiropractics has been recognized by the International Chiropractors Association. I took part in a symposium on national fitness in March 2004 in Columbus, Ohio, with California Gov. Arnold Schwarzenegger.

Work Pays Off

The accolades came pouring in for me in 1988, when I rushed for a team-record 1,502 yards. My best day came on a 95-degree October day in Anaheim, when my conditioning really paid off.

We defeated the Rams 24-21 and I scored all three of our touchdowns, while gaining 190 yards on 24 carries. Probably the play I'm most associated with was a 46-yard scoring run in which it seemed like I bounced off just about every Rams defensive player on the field.

Afterward, Rams coach John Robinson called me "the best runner in the league." That was pretty high praise because Robinson had coached Eric Dickerson, and Dickerson was still in his prime with the Indianapolis Colts. It was also extremely flattering because I considered myself a lot more than just a "runner."

That season I gained 2,036 total yards, nearly 35 percent of the 49ers' entire yardage for the season. *Sports Illustrated* bestowed its NFL Most Valuable Player on me, while The Associated Press honored me as NFL Offensive Player of the Year.

Keep Calling Us Finesse

Through most of my career, there seemed to be a perception around the league and in the media that the 49ers were a finesse football team.

In many ways, that label worked to our advantage because our opponents were not prepared for the physical brand of football we played. We had some players on our team who would take your head off.

Guys like Carlton Williamson, Eric Wright, Ronnie Lott, Jeff Fuller, "Hacksaw" Reynolds and Riki Ellison were highly competitive and tough as nails. It's laughable to think any team with those guys would be considered a finesse team.

We also had a bunch of unsung heroes who were blue-collar performers. Ron Ferrari, Bill Ring, Milt McColl and Rick Gervais ... These were all guys who fit their particular roles and played great special teams. That's how we worked. We were a machine.

Coach Walsh tried to play up that image of us being a finesse football team because he knew it only helped us in the long run if teams came into games against us expecting anything but a physical, smash-mouth kind of battle.

Rivalry with the Giants

We had some intense games against the Chicago Bears and Washington Redskins, but the intensity of the games we had against the New York Giants was difficult to match. Even the contrasts in our coaches helped add to the rivalry. Bill Parcells was coming into his own as a coach. He was known as a hard-nosed, quick-tempered man who emphasized a smash-mouth mentality, while Coach Walsh was seen as a refined intellectual who would often outprepare and outwit his opponents.

Even the physical differences—Parcells, big and round; Walsh, fit and tan—between those two men only added to the intrigue of when our teams met on the playing field. It was a big-time rivalry, and all I know is they hated us and we hated them.

I had my personal battles against Giants linebacker Harry Carson. In a Monday night game in 1984, I embarrassed him on national television. I juked him after I caught a pass. He went one way and I went the other way to score a touchdown.

Carson did not forget that play. A couple years later, they beat us 49-3 in the playoffs. I was battling injuries all season, and in that game, Carson and Lawrence Taylor high-lowed me and put me out of the game. I remember he was talking a lot during that game.

Heck, even their fans had a chance to rub our noses in it. After the game, we were all looking forward to getting on a plane and getting home, but there were about 5,000 Giants fans outside the stadium in the Meadowlands. They wouldn't let our bus leave, and then they started rocking the bus.

Hey, your team just beat us 49-3. Isn't that enough? Just let us go to the airport, so you can go home to your families.

The next year Harry Carson wrote a book, and he had a whole chapter about me, which was flattering—sort of. But it was also more than a little disturbing to read how he described a particular tackle on me.

"Craig put his head down and tried to bull his way over," Carson wrote. "There was a solid collision. The hit I made on Craig was like having an orgasm."

Yikes. You can see why those words still haunt me 20 years later.

Whenever I'd go to the Pro Bowl and see Harry, we were cool. Lawrence Taylor and I are good friends. He plays in my golf tournament every year. He cracks me up. He is definitely a piece of work. I remember when he'd tackle me, he'd be chirping, "Son, you got to be a little tougher. You can't bring it like that."

Prepared for the Cold

One of the more memorable games we played was in the 1988 NFC championship game when we went to Soldier Field and played the Bears in so-called "Bear weather."

Everybody was saying the 49ers could not deal with cold weather because we were sissies—or whatever else derogatory term they might have been calling us.

I remember how Coach Walsh made us visualize what it would be like to play in extremely cold conditions. He talked about the field being frozen. He talked about the leather football feeling hard and frozen in our hands. He told us we had to hold onto the ball just a little bit tighter.

The entire week as we prepared in comfortable weather at our practice facility in Santa Clara, we talked about playing in cold weather and got mentally prepared for it. When we arrived in Chicago, we were ready to rock and roll. As it turned out, the Bears weren't ready for their own cold weather.

The game-time temperatures were in the teens and the wind chill was 26 degrees below zero. The field was so hard we did not wear cleats because there wasn't any traction. We wore tennis shoes because there would be less slipping and sliding.

Every time I got tackled it was like falling on a sidewalk with sharp edges of concrete sticking up. At the end of the game, my arms were all cut up from the ice and frozen grass. Obviously, these were not pleasant playing conditions.

So what kept us going? We knew if we played hard for three hours we'd be in sunny Miami for the Super Bowl. That's what kept us going. That's what motivated us. We went out and took it to the Bears. Jerry Rice caught a 61-yard touchdown pass from Joe Montana in the first quarter, and nothing could stop us in a 28-3 victory.

Bears Weather?

Three weeks later, I played in the Pro Bowl in Hawaii, which was a long way from that frozen Sunday at Soldier Field.

The Bears' Mike Ditka coached the NFC Pro Bowl team because his team lost in the NFC championship game. Both of us were glad to be in Honolulu, where it was typically beautiful weather.

I wanted to talk to Ditka about playing in that kind of weather. "Tell me something," I said to him. "How do you prepare for that kind of cold? How do you practice in that stuff?"

He told me, "Roger, you can't prepare for it. I was just like you. I was counting down the seconds until that game was over. I was just trying to get it over with."

Road Warriors

The victory over the Bears was just another example of what made us such a good team away from Candlestick Park, our home stadium. Just consider, in 10 seasons from 1981 to '90, we compiled a .809 win percentage on the road, while winning just .671 of our home games.

Coach Walsh had a way of making us feel as if we were this army that was going into someone else's territory. It was just us. It was Us against The World.

When adversity hit, we knew we had to rally among ourselves and keep fighting. That kind of unity made us come together as a team. A lot of times, when you're playing at home, you relax because you know everyone in the stands is on your side.

Typically, Coach Walsh would begin his sermons about road trips in the preseason and continue to emphasize the importance of playing well away from home as the season went on. The nucleus of his teams remained intact, so those players continued to set the tone for the newcomers.

Coach Walsh recently talked about the emphasis he placed on winning road games: "We spoke of it, addressed it, we discussed it week after week after week, even before the season started. It was 50 of us vs. 50,000 of them. I used axioms and experiences I read about in warfare, where troops were backed up and they had nowhere to go. We went in with a vengeance and all we had was each other."

We won an NFL-record 19 consecutive road games, including that playoff victory over the Bears, from 1988 through the

1990 season. I was no longer with the 49ers in 1991, when they lost their first road game of the season to end the streak.

In the last five seasons, entering the 2004 season, the 49ers were 25-15 (.625) at home and 14-26 (.350) on the road. In the future, the 49ers would be wise to place the same kind of emphasis on road games Coach Walsh did.

We would always use the same routine for road games. We would arrive at the team hotel around 11 p.m. on Friday nights and have dinner together as a team before going to bed.

On Saturday mornings we would have breakfast and meetings before going to the stadium for an hour-long walk-through practice. Then we'd meet again in the evening and Coach Walsh would put on a highlight film of the previous week's game—if it was a victory.

It was always motivating to watch that film. Coach Walsh was big into visualizing positive thoughts, and he wanted us to see ourselves doing great things the night before a game.

Chapter 3

THE 49ER
FAMILY

I n my eight seasons with the 49ers, I played with a lot of Hall of Fame players and many others who are deserving of the honor.

The 49ers of the 1980s were an All-Star team. Heck, we had two Hall of Fame quarterbacks on the roster at the same time. That was quite a luxury, of course, but it also created some tension.

The whole Joe Montana vs. Steve Young controversy was all anybody talked about in the San Francisco Bay Area for several years. It was a difficult time to be in the locker room, but in many ways it helped galvanize the team. It made us stronger because we knew both players could do the job when called upon.

Whenever Joe went down with an injury, we knew Steve would step in and keep us moving in a positive direction. That is what was expected out of him. Heck, that is what was expected out of every backup on that roster. Steve Young was not unique in that sense.

There was a belief on our team that whenever the starter could not play, the backup was going to be just as good or better for as long as he had to play. And the team rallied around those players.

That is why we had backup quarterbacks such as Jeff Kemp, Mike Moroski, Matt Cavanaugh and Steve Bono step up and rescue the team when we needed to win a game or two. Those quarterbacks knew the system would take care of them. They played within themselves and had the benefit of some great coaches like Dennis Green, Mike Holmgren, Paul Hackett and later Mike Shanahan and Gary Kubiak. Those quarterbacks were going back to school and taking a class in West Coast Offense 101.

And it wasn't just the quarterbacks who excelled when needed. It was everybody.

Mike Wilson, a backup receiver, was somebody you could count on. He didn't want to take the glory. He was a role player and he knew his role. If he was asked to play a role in only two plays a game, he would make sure he was prepared for those two plays. He made things happen when the ball was thrown his way, and he never cried about not getting enough playing time.

Dana McLemore was a dangerous punt returner who did not get a lot of attention, but who still holds team records with four career touchdowns, most punt return yards and highest career average from 1982 to '87.

And there were many others on defense who laid it all on the line for the team.

Guys like Ron Ferrari, Rick Gervais, Milt McColl and Mike Walter did whatever it took to help the team. In the mid-1980s, we got invaluable contributions from a bunch of wily veterans, guys like Lawrence Pillars and Willie Harper. Those guys set an example for the younger players.

Coach Walsh did a masterful job of acquiring older players from other organizations to help for a brief period of time. In 1984, he traded for defensive linemen Louie Kelcher, Manu

Tuiasosopo and Gary "Big Hands" Johnson, and in 1986, he added running back Joe Cribbs.

Even after Coach Walsh left, the tradition continued, with linebacker Matt Millen playing on a Super Bowl team. He came to the organization as a role player and became a quasi-coach.

That is why this section is called "The 49ers Family." Everybody played a role in the franchise's ascent to its fabled position of "Team of the '80s."

Joe Montana

Joe was like a Green Beret. There was never any player, any team or any situation that scared this man. It didn't matter what kind of adversity surrounded him; he always made the best of the situation.

He had many memorable performances in his career, but none was as impressive as the game he pulled out in 1989 against the Philadelphia Eagles.

The Eagles sacked him eight times and knocked him out of the game briefly in the second quarter. We were down 28-17 with seven minutes to play against one of the game's best defenses, which featured Reggie White, Jerome Brown, Clyde Simmons, Seth Joyner and Wes Hopkins.

But Joe threw four touchdown passes in the fourth quarter for an exhilarating 38-28 victory. He earned the respect of a great defense with that win.

He was never going to give up or give in. He was like a surgeon, the way he dissected defenses. Joe knew how to get rid of the ball on time and get the ball into the hands of guys who could make plays.

When St. Louis's Kurt Warner was at the top of his game, he used the system to his advantage in much the same way. Brett Favre is another quarterback who has a little bit of Montana in

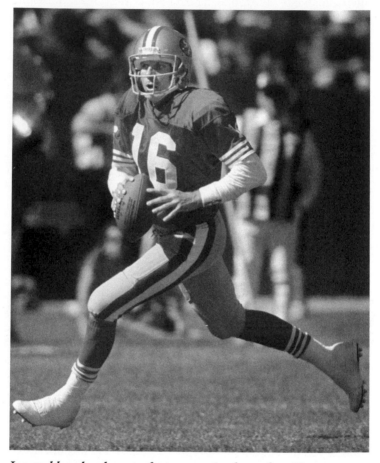

Joe could make plays on the move or in the pocket. He was a master at going through his progression of receivers and finding the open man. (Photo by Brad Mangin)

him. But sometimes Brett holds onto the ball too long and forces passes when it is not necessary.

New England's Tom Brady probably reminds me more of Joe than anyone else playing the game. When he came back to the Bay Area around Christmas prior to his first season in the playoffs, I talked to him. I told Tom that it is important to get his teammates to believe every time they step onto the field they are going to win that day. I told him he needed to work on being consistent, so he would continue to bring his team back year after year. He has a lot of the same characteristics as Joe. His team rallies around him, and he knows how to win. Tom Brady also shows that same calmness under pressure as Joe. He really has a chance to be the next Joe Montana during a time when the NFL is starved for great quarterbacks.

Joe, the Prankster

To a list of Joe Montana's many talents, you can add "bicycle thief."

During training camp, we would use bicycles to make the trip from one side of campus to the other. We needed our bikes because the dormitories were on one side of the campus and the locker room and meeting rooms were on the other side. Everything was spread out all over the place on the Sierra College campus.

After a long practice or meeting, everybody would look forward to getting back to our rooms to stretch out and rest. But with Joe around, things were never that easy. He would hide bikes all over the place.

Some bikes would end up in the spruce trees on campus; others would be found on the low roofs of the classrooms. You'd come out of a meeting around 10 p.m. and be looking around for your bike. A lot of 49ers players in the 1980s had to make that walk all the way back to the dorm rooms because Joe put their bikes out of reach—but not out of sight.

Steve Young

Steve Young turned out to be one of the great quarterbacks in 49ers team history. I have a great deal of respect for the way he constantly worked on his game to get better year after year after year. Steve might have been as physically gifted as any quarterback to ever play the game.

The funny thing is, Steve was not a great quarterback when he came to the 49ers. He was molded into a great quarterback after he got here. It was almost like he was a running back playing out of position.

When Steve broke into professional football in 1984, he caused quite a stir because of the magnitude of the contract he signed with the Los Angeles Express of the USFL. His 15-page contract detailed that he would get paid $40.1 million for 43 years, with more than $34.5 million of the deal being paid over 37 years in an annuity. The final payment of $3.173 million is scheduled to be delivered by 2027.

In the USFL, Steve was known for two things: his contract and his running. He became the first player in pro football history to pass for 300 yards and rush for 100 in the same game. He even played one game at running back for the Express.

Steve exercised a clause in his contract to get a release from the Express and moved on to the Tampa Bay Buccaneers in 1985. In two seasons with the Bucs, he compiled a miserable 3-16 record.

Three weeks before the 1987 draft, the Bucs announced the signing of Vinny Testaverde, whose selection as the No. 1 overall pick was a clear signal Steve was no longer wanted in Tampa Bay.

Coach Walsh wanted Steve with the 49ers, so the coach/general manager combined second- and fourth-round draft picks with a lump of Eddie DeBartolo's cash to acquire Young in a trade.

Steve had to learn to play quarterback like he had never been forced to play before. He had to learn how to sit in the pocket and be a quarterback in the West Coast system. Once he settled down, he became one of the most efficient quarterbacks in the history of the game, recording a passer rating of better than 100 in four consecutive seasons.

Steve Young had to learn he was not getting paid to run the ball with the 49ers. He became a great quarterback after spending some time in the system and watching Joe Montana. (Photo by Brad Mangin)

He also had to learn he could not keep getting hit and put-ting the team in jeopardy. Sooner or later that's going to catch up to you. If the team is banking on you being there, you can't be running around and getting injured.

Steve had to do a lot of studying, and he had to understand you have three reads on every pass play. Early on, it was sort of scary because Steve would just take off running.

I played with Steve a lot when Joe was hurt, and a lot of times he wouldn't even throw me that short pass because he wanted to run the ball. I could have protected him from a lot of hits. Joe was always smart. He would dump that ball off to me so I would take the punishment, not him.

But later on, Steve started using the back more. Ricky Watters caught 66 passes in 1994 when Steve got more familiar with the offense. It's not exactly a coincidence the 49ers won the Super Bowl that year.

Joe vs. Steve

I looked at Steve Young as a colt just wanting to run, and the 49ers had to put the reins on him. He wanted to show his stuff. And Joe Montana was the old veteran quarterback who had been around and paid his dues, and he wasn't ready to take a back seat to anybody.

The 49ers had two highly competitive quarterbacks. Joe was the starter; and Steve wanted his job. Joe knew Steve wanted his job, and that was the makings of the quarterback controversy.

There was a rivalry going on in practice for repetitions and in games for playing time. From 1987 to '92, Joe and Steve were on the same team. There weren't any big arguments between them, but you could certainly feel the tension.

There were times when Mike Holmgren, our offensive coordinator, had to pull Steve away from the team to walk him around and cool him down. Steve wanted to play. Joe had never had anybody challenge him for his job. Let's just say it wasn't the most pleasant place to be.

But, ultimately, I think competition within the team helped both players. When Joe got hurt, Steve came in and showed his stuff. He wanted to show everybody he was capable of taking the job and running with it.

After our tough loss to Minnesota in the 1987 playoffs, the controversy really started. Through the entire off season, the debate was whether Joe or Steve should be the 49ers' starter in 1988.

They had equal opportunities during training camp of 1988, but it was Joe who was named the starter for the season opener against New Orleans. After a narrow victory, Coach Walsh made a surprise announcement: Steve would start the next game at the Meadowlands against the New York Giants because Montana was not completely healthy.

Steve Young and Joe Montana always kept tabs on each other. Here they are during the 1988 training camp in Rocklin. (Photo by Brad Mangin)

Steve struggled, and Joe came to the rescue. He pulled out a 20-17 victory when he hit Jerry Rice on a 78-yard scoring pass in the final minute of the game. With Joe leading the way, we went on to win two straight Super Bowls.

Steve never felt accepted by the 49ers fans because everybody loved Joe so much. After all, Joe was the Golden Boy. I felt bad for Steve because he got booed a lot. But eventually Steve earned everyone's respect by winning the Super Bowl after the 1994 season.

Steve Young developed a good command of the offense after taking over the full-time starting job. He built up a solid rapport with Jerry Rice, which helped the 49ers cruise to an easy win in Super Bowl XXIX. (Photo by Brad Mangin)

George Seifert

George Seifert was an interesting guy. He was very quiet and introverted off the field. He even showed a very stoic demeanor on the sideline, but when he got worked up, he was a Tasmanian devil. He was never afraid to get in your face if you screwed up.

In his own way, George was a genius. He built those great 49ers defenses of the 1980s. His defenses were fast and hard-hitting. He and Ray Rhodes did a great job getting their guys prepared to play.

George always had very good schemes and game plans for the defense, and I don't think he got nearly enough credit for that. Championships are won with defense, and George was the defensive coordinator for two of those Super Bowl-winning teams.

As a head coach, George was definitely underrated. He took over in 1989 season from Coach Walsh. It was still Walsh's team, but George kept everything going in the same direction. He resisted the temptation to make changes just for the sake of making changes.

He finally carved out his own niche with the 49ers in 1994, when he came under intense pressure to return the 49ers to the mountaintop. George was able to overcome the Dallas Cowboys in the NFC championship game and win the Super Bowl with Steve Young at quarterback.

When he left the 49ers after the 1996 season, George had the highest winning percentage (.755) of any coach in NFL history with a 108-35 record. But after spending three seasons with the Carolina Panthers, George dropped to seventh among coaches with 100 or more victories.

George is a well rounded person and does not need to be in the spotlight as a head coach. Although he is very competitive, I'm guessing he's had no problem adjusting to his retired life as a roaming fisherman.

Superstitious George

George was probably the most superstitious man I've ever known. One of his superstitions was that he only referred to his superstitions as "quirks." He had so many of these quirks it was difficult to keep track of them all.

The 49ers' practice facility used to have one artificial surface field with a big 49ers helmet logo at the 50-yard line. For whatever reason, George would never walk on that helmet under any circumstances. When Steve Mariucci took over as head coach in 1997, he held his first press briefing on the helmet—something George was probably physically incapable of doing.

George also had this thing with his breath mints. He'd blow on them three times before popping one into his mouth. Before games, he would take a lap around the locker room without his shirt on.

He also had to arrange his napkin and silverware in a specific fashion before eating. And he always ate Chinese food on Tuesday.

George also had his special articles of clothing that enabled him to live life with fewer worries. When he forgot to pack his lucky blue sweater for the trip to New Orleans for Super Bowl XXIV, the players sent home for it and presented it to him as a gift. It must've worked, because we won that game quite easily.

A few years after I left the team, George was grinding his teeth so badly during a playoff game in Green Bay that he asked the equipment staff to get him a mouthpiece that he wore during the game. That was the final game George coached with the 49ers.

Carmen Policy

Carmen Policy, with his sharp suits and even sharper tongue, was a great ambassador for the team. While practicing law in Youngstown, Ohio, Carmen became a 49ers vice president and general counsel in 1983.

In 1989, after Coach Walsh was stripped of his president responsibilities, Carmen moved to the Bay Area to become the organization's executive vice president. He represented the 49ers at all league matters and functions.

Carmen really knows how to work a room. He connected with influential people in the community and around the league and made Eddie DeBartolo look good. Eddie had his rough spots, and Carmen had a knack for smoothing things over.

Eddie never cared about networking with other owners around the league other than being friends with Al Davis and Jerry Jones. I guess mavericks find a way to stick together. But Carmen was the politician of the organization.

In 1993, when the league devised its salary cap as a way of preventing the 49ers from continuing to be the New York Yankees of the NFL, Carmen devised methods for manipulating the cap. In 1994, he was named NFL Executive of the Year.

Of course, Carmen and Eddie, who were longtime friends, had a falling-out, and Carmen became a minority owner in the expansion Cleveland Browns in 1998. Since his departure, the 49ers have changed their philosophy in dealing with the salary cap.

Instead of spending whatever it takes and manipulating the cap without much regard for the future of the organization, the 49ers now believe the way to function is to tackle the cap conservatively and try to maintain a consistent product on the field from year to year.

John McVay

One of the true unsung heroes of the 49ers through the decades is John McVay, who finally retired from his front office role after the 2004 draft.

Originally, John came to the 49ers in 1979 when Coach Walsh was hired. Among his various roles were: vice president and general manager, director of player personnel, director of football operations, vice president for football administration, administrative vice president, and assistant to the president.

During his time with the organization, the 49ers won all five Super Bowls. He was named *The Sporting News'* NFL Executive of the Year in 1989, after the club's fourth Super Bowl title.

John retired in 1995, but he did not get too comfortable in his life after football before the 49ers came calling for him to return.

Carmen Policy left for Cleveland in 1998, and Dwight Clark would soon follow. So John came out of retirement as a favor to Eddie DeBartolo, who thought he would be getting his team back after his legal problems were cleared up.

For a while, John McVay was the only football executive in the building. He came back to the 49ers and had to spearhead the effort to deal with the salary cap mess Carmen and Dwight left behind.

When Dr. John and Denise York took control of the team, John McVay remained with the 49ers' front office—extending his contract one year at a time. He was always supposed to be a part-time employee, but it seemed like he worked as many hours as everybody else.

So now, John is back to the retired life. But don't be surprised if the 49ers get in a bit of a pickle and need him to again ride his white horse to the rescue.

Ronnie Lott

Sure, Ronnie Lott is in the Hall of Fame, and he is considered one of the greatest defensive players of all time. But I'm telling you he did not get his just due.

He was a great, great player and a great, great leader. Ronnie played the game with otherworldly instincts. He had a knack for knowing where the play was going, and he had the physical tools to get there and do something about it.

Ronnie played every position in the defensive backfield and made it to the Pro Bowl in each spot. He played cornerback, strong safety and free safety. He could adapt to any position you put him in.

He made a lot of great hits in his career, including a bone-jarring tackle of Cincinnati's Ickey Woods early in our Super Bowl victory in Miami that helped set the tone for the game. But I remember one hit he put on Atlanta's Gerald Riggs, in which he smashed into him and turned him sideways.

Ronnie was fearless. He would crash his body into people, and a lot of times Ronnie did not get up. But he would never back down. He would come at the ball carrier just as hard the next time.

His leadership skills were nonpareil. In 1985, we were in a tight game against the Los Angeles Rams. Our defense was fantastic, and our offense was sputtering with a few three-and-outs.

When he was coming off the field, he got in my face and started screaming at me, "All I want is four yards a crack, Rog! You got that, Rog? All I want is four yards!"

That got me mad. I thought, "I'm going to show him that I can get a lot more than four yards."

Joe threw me a little swing pass—22 Z-In—to the right side. The Rams had defensive end Jack Youngblood in coverage against me, and Joe lofted the pass perfectly over him. I made two people miss and I went down the field 73 yards for a touchdown. When I got back to the sideline, I was yelling at Ronnie, "Is that good enough for you, Ronnie?"

That was the kind of player Ronnie was. He found a way to get his teammates motivated. We won that game 28-14, and Ronnie's challenge to me clearly accomplished its goal.

Sacrifice for the Team

The quintessential Ronnie Lott story involves the pinkie on his left hand.

In the final game of the 1985 regular season, Ronnie went in to make a tackle on Dallas running back Timmy Newsome. His pinkie got caught between his shoulder pad and Newsome's helmet. The bone at the tip of the pinkie was crushed.

Ronnie continued to play—in excruciating pain—with the shattered bone. Admittedly, he did not have his best game in the first round of the playoffs when we lost 17-3 to the New York Giants.

After his pinkie failed to heal properly through the first part of the off season, Ronnie decided to have the tip of his little finger amputated to ensure he would be ready to start the 1986 season.

That pinkie is a symbol of the dedication to the game and to each other that typified the 49ers of the 1980s. It now serves as a teaching tool to his kids, who look at it with much curiosity.

When he was recently asked how he explains his odd-looking pinkie to his children, Ronnie got emotional.

"You just joke around with them, let them know that there are certain things that happen in your life," he said, wiping tears from his eyes. "You try to explain to them that there are sacrifices that you make and sometimes people don't understand them.

"My kids right now, for all they know, it looks like E.T.'s head. But at some point they'll get it. That's what I'm hoping, that at some point in their lives, they'll be able to make sacrifices for their teammates, for their friends. It's kind of hard to get people to understand why you would do that. But at the end of the day, it's all worth it."

Ronnie Lott was all business from the minute he stepped onto the playing field. He might be the best defensive player in the history of the league. (Photo by Brad Mangin)

Eric Wright

If it weren't for a serious groin injury that cut short his football career, Eric Wight might be regarded as one of the best cover cornerbacks to ever play the game. He was that good.

He made the Pro Bowl two times, but he easily could have been selected two or three more times if it weren't for his injury. There is no doubt in my mind he was on a path to the Hall of Fame before he went down with the problems that limited him from 1985 to the end of his career in 1990.

Later, everybody talked about how Deion Sanders could take care of half the field and teams were afraid to challenge him. That's how it was with Eric. Nobody wanted to even try to test Eric Wright.

In a lot of ways, Eric was ahead of his time. Teams are looking to combat today's big receivers with bigger, more physical cornerbacks. When he was drafted, he was six foot one, 180 pounds. That was big for a cornerback, and he filled out from there.

When the 49ers took him in the second round of the 1981 draft and he was successful, it began a trend. The organization started looking for tall, lanky cornerbacks to fit the "Eric Wright" mold.

The 49ers were thinking along those lines in 2002 when they selected cornerback Mike Rumph in the first round. Mike struggled as a rookie, but it looks as if he is going to develop into a pretty good cover man as he gains more and more experience.

Carlton Williamson

We had some guys in our secondary who could hit. Carlton Williamson, who started six seasons at strong safety, was as good as it gets when it came to dishing out some punishment.

I remember one time in practice, he hit me so hard I thought my chest was going to cave in. He was big, and he packed quite a wallop when he got a good running start from his spot in the secondary.

Carlton was part of that incredible backfield of 1981 that won the Super Bowl with three rookies. He was a third-round draft pick out of the University of Pittsburgh in '81.

We called Carlton "The Hammer" because he looked like Fred Williamson, the former All-Pro player with the Oakland Raiders and Kansas City Chiefs who later went on to announce a season on *Monday Night Football* with Howard Cosell.

Dwight Hicks

On that first Super Bowl title team, Dwight Hicks was the old man of the secondary. He came to the team in 1979 and started four games at free safety, sharing time there with Tony Dungy.

He started every game in 1980 and then was joined by that incredible rookie class in '81 that included Ronnie Lott, Eric Wright and Carlton Williamson. Together, those guys became known as "Dwight Hicks and the Hot Licks." Pretty catchy name, huh?

Dwight helped keep those young guys together. He was pretty talented, and those rookies looked up to him. He also set the tone with a strong work ethic. Dwight made the Pro Bowl four times during his career, and he made a lot of big plays.

Just like everybody else in that defensive backfield, Dwight was not afraid to hit. I think Ronnie learned a lot from him early in his career.

Jeff Fuller

Probably the most athletic of all the guys in the secondary of those teams I played with was Jeff Fuller. He was 230 pounds and could run, cover and tackle. He was smooth and could do it all. He was a very special defensive back.

Jeff became the starter in 1987 at strong safety, replacing Carlton Williamson. He had several good seasons until the seventh game of the 1989 season, when his career ended and his life changed dramatically.

We were playing in Stanford Stadium on October 22, 1989, because the Loma Prieta earthquake had closed Candlestick Park for repairs. All of us had great memories of playing at Stanford because of our win over the Dolphins in Super Bowl XIX. But now, when I drive past that place, the first thing I think about is what happened to Jeff Fuller.

New England running back John Stephens took a pitch and started right. Our inside linebacker, Jim Fahnhorst, grabbed Stephens by the legs. Jeff came up from his safety position and made a hit on Stephens that produced a sickening "whack."

Jeff was not able to get up. I remember being on the sideline, pleading, "Come on, Jeff, get up ... get up!"

But Jeff could not move. They had to bring an ambulance onto the field to transport him to Stanford Hospital, which was right there on campus.

Even though we won the game, Coach George Seifert was very downcast when he addressed the team afterward. It sure didn't feel like we had won the game, that's for sure.

Jeff sustained a crushed neck, and he would never play football again. Today, he can walk and get around, but one arm is paralyzed. Coach Walsh, who had retired after the previous season, orchestrated an annuity for Jeff, and Eddie DeBartolo put it together. The annuity pays Jeff $100,000 every year for the rest of his life.

Ray Wersching

Through the years, the 49ers have experienced more than their fair share of problems at the kicker position. The last 49ers kicker who could be counted on to perform year in and year out was Ray Wersching.

Even as field goal percentages are rising around the league, Ray remains the most accurate kicker in team history. Part of the problem with being a 49ers kicker is the unenviable task of trying to negotiate those tricky conditions at Candlestick Park.

Ray Wersching was the last reliable kicker to suit up for the 49ers. He somehow managed to maintain his confidence while kicking at windy Candlestick Park. (Photo by Brad Mangin)

As he recently said, "It's difficult to kick in Candlestick. It's a mental thing. As the season wears on, the weather gets worse and worse, and the field gets muddier, and you have to cope with the wind."

Ray never seemed to get bothered by any of that because of his unique routine. He would never look up at the goal posts upon trotting onto the field. Today, kickers are always looking at the flags atop the uprights to factor the wind into their kicks. But Ray tried to remain oblivious to the conditions at Candlestick.

Ray would jog onto the field, pat holder Joe Montana on his shoulder and say, "Help me." It must have worked. He made 72.8 percent of his field goal attempts from 1977 to '87. Oddly, he made 74 percent of his attempts at Candlestick.

Jerry Rice

When the 49ers selected Jerry in the first round of the 1985 draft out of Mississippi Valley State, it was a case of the small-town guy coming to the big city. I knew this could be overwhelming to him.

That's why I took him under my wing. He wasn't very friendly with anyone. I don't think at that stage in his life he was comfortable around people. He was introverted, and I sensed that and tried to make him one of the guys.

During his rookie season he went through some difficult times. He dropped a lot of passes and was clearly pressing a lot. We hung out a few times, and I tried to be with him as much as possible. He shared some things with me, and we had a brotherly relationship.

When Jerry Rice came to the 49ers, I took it upon myself to take him under my wing and get him acclimated to life in the NFL. (Photo by Brad Mangin)

Things really started to change for Jerry around midseason when he became more and more comfortable with his surroundings. We had a Monday night game late in the season against the Los Angeles Rams, and he shocked everybody.

He caught 10 passes for 214 yards in front of a national television audience. He averaged 18.9 yards a catch and totaled 927 yards as a rookie. That's when I knew he was for real and would have a great career.

Now, of course, Jerry owns every significant NFL receiving record. He is a physical marvel, playing the receiver position well into his 40s. The league will probably never see another receiver quite like Jerry Rice.

Jerry Rice, the greatest receiver in the history of the NFL, scores one of his league-record touchdowns on a leaping catch against San Diego in 1991. (Photo by Brad Mangin)

Lindsy McLean

The NFL locker room is a melting pot. During my time with the 49ers, our locker room was probably more diverse than any in the league.

Of course, we had players from every imaginable background and upbringing. We never had any problems with black and white. Inside the locker room, we were all brothers.

That included our trainer, Lindsy McLean.

Lindsy was among the first people Coach Walsh hired when he took over in 1979. Lindsy continued working for the 49ers until July of 2003. It wasn't until six months after his retirement that Lindsy shared with the world what we already knew: He is gay.

That's right, the 49ers' head athletic trainer was gay, and it certainly did not make any difference to me or most of the players on those teams. He was part of the family, and he is a great guy.

I know Lindsy endured some difficult times with some of the 49ers players in the 1990s, but he proved to be a much bigger man than those people who tried to intimidate him.

Lindsy was a great trainer and someone who earned everybody's trust, which is essential in a trainer. Lindsy and I would always go through the same routine every time he taped my ankles. After he was finished, he would always tap my ankle three times for luck.

We certainly treated him with as much respect as anyone else in the locker room while I was with the team. To my knowledge, there weren't any players in that locker room who were homophobic or who felt uncomfortable around Lindsy.

Because all of the veterans on the team respected Lindsy, it showed the way for the younger players. I can tell you one thing, if we'd seen any of the younger guys discriminating against Lindsy, there would have been hell to pay from Joe, Ronnie or me. We would've kicked their butts.

Renaldo Nehemiah

Renaldo Nehemiah, one of the great high hurdlers of all time, played three seasons for the 49ers, and we were teammates for two years. It was a thrill to be teammates with Renaldo because of my appreciation of track and field.

Of course, Renaldo had great straight-ahead speed—world-class speed, in fact. He had great form as a runner, but it was difficult for him to change direction, make cuts and run patterns.

We used to call him "Noodles" because of the way his legs looked when he ran patterns. He was so fast it made his legs look wobbly.

His best season was in 1984, when he caught 18 passes and averaged 19.8 yards. I think Renaldo was on the verge of becoming a very good receiver in the NFL, but then his career changed dramatically after he was knocked out on a brutal hit against the Atlanta Falcons. He had never played football, and he was not prepared for that kind of punishment. I wish I could've taken that hit, because I knew what it would take to get up from something like that and not be affected. I knew Renaldo would never be the same after that. He did not come back for the '85 season. Today, he is the most prominent agent for track athletes in the country.

Jeff Stover

Coach Walsh was bold in molding track athletes into football players. He tried it with Renaldo Nehemiah, and he had quite a bit of success with former weight men Jeff Stover and Michael Carter.

Jeff put together a solid career with the 49ers that lasted seven seasons before it was cut short because of injuries. But how Jeff even made it to the NFL was a remarkable testament to Walsh's vision as a coach and talent evaluator.

Jeff was a fullback in a single-wing offense at Corning Union High School in Northern California. Walsh, then the Stanford coach, saw him play in an All-Star game and was blown away.

After the game, Coach Walsh introduced himself to Jeff and offered him a full scholarship on the spot. But Jeff told him he had already accepted a track scholarship to the University of Oregon.

"You're wasting your time," Coach Walsh told him. "You should be playing football."

But Jeff did not play football for the Ducks. He threw the shot put and discus and did not get a chance to go to the Olympics because of America's boycott of the 1980 Moscow Olympics.

A couple years later, Jeff wanted to get back into football. He arranged a tryout for Walsh, who was now the coach of the 49ers. Coach Walsh signed him and turned him into a very productive defensive end.

Michael Carter

Every defensive line needs some bulk in the middle to stuff the run, and that is why Michael Carter was so valuable to the team from 1984 to '92.

Michael was the anchor of those great defensive lines. It took three men to keep him out of the offensive backfield, so that allowed our linebackers to roam free and make tackles. He was always willing to sacrifice for the good of the team.

Michael is also another one of my former teammates who experienced a lot of success in track and field. As a member of the U.S. Olympic team in 1984, Michael won a silver medal in the shot put.

Even today, a quarter-century later, Michael holds the U.S. high school record with a throw of 81 feet, three and a half inches in the shot put from his days at Jefferson High School in Dallas. In 2002, Michael's daughter, Michelle, set the Texas state high school record with a throw of 53 feet, three and three-quarters inches, just four inches behind the national record.

Charles Haley

Charles Haley is at the top of the list of real characters with whom I played during my career.

He was a grown man, but he acted like a little kid. He had conflicts with everyone. Charles would come up to people with the sole purpose of nagging them. He'd stick something in your ear or he'd give you a "snuggy" without any warning. A lot of times, other guys just didn't have the patience to deal with him.

Leading up to our Super Bowl against the Denver Broncos, nose tackle Jim Burt had had enough. Those two men got into a heated scuffle at the team's practice facility. A lot of times when teammates get into fights, it can tear a team apart. But when Charles was involved, it was really no big deal. It was just two guys blowing off a little steam. Charles never messed with Jim Burt again.

Another time, Charles provoked Jerry Rice to the point where things almost got ugly. After being subjected to Charles a bit too long, Jerry picked up a fire extinguisher and went after him. Fortunately, that was one fire that was put out before things got too hot.

Yep, Charles had a certain way of getting under people's skin. The more you showed that it bothered you, the more relentless he would become. He never really messed with me because I just laughed him off and never took him too seriously.

Charles's personality eventually became too much for everybody in the organization. Even though he was still one of the dominant pass rushers in the NFL, Coach Seifert just couldn't take it any more. The 49ers traded Charles to the Dallas Cowboys in 1992 for a couple of lower draft picks that really did not amount to anything.

Meanwhile, Charles continued tormenting the 49ers. He made the 49ers pay for trading him. The Cowboys beat up on the 49ers for a few seasons, and Charles was the reason why. He was the marquee player on the Cowboys' defense during their run of three Super Bowl titles over a four-year stretch. Charles owns five Super Bowls rings, two of them from our days with the 49ers.

Keena Turner

When I think about guys who embody the 49ers spirit, the name Keena Turner comes to mind.

He was a very talented player who had a great career despite the fact he was small for his position. He weighed only about 215 pounds at most, and he was playing outside linebacker. But he was so fast nobody could even think about running sweeps to his side.

He played injured through his later years with the 49ers, but I'll always remember a vicious hit he made on New York Giants running back Ottis Anderson. Exhibiting his great speed, Keena came out of nowhere in pursuit of Anderson and hit him in the facemask, dropping Anderson as if he had been leveled by a sledgehammer.

He played 11 seasons for the 49ers, from 1980 to '90, and now he works for the organization as director of player development and coordinator of the alumni functions.

Jack "Hacksaw" Reynolds

Hacksaw had a tremendous impact on a lot of the players who would eventually carry on the 49ers' tradition to others. Ronnie Lott recently described his first team meeting back in 1981 when Coach Walsh told all the players to take notes.

Ronnie admits he wasn't properly prepared. However, Hacksaw's preparedness and dedication set an example for the rookie.

"Hacksaw had a hundred pencils, and I asked him for one," Lott remembered. "Hacksaw looked at me and said, 'If you want to be a champion, you won't forget to bring a pencil.' I say, 'OK, but can I have a pencil?' and he says, 'No.'

"That moment told me a lot about who he is and why he was a champion. It told me a lot about the game of football—that it was not just going out there and playing. You had to study the game, you had a responsibility to the game. That one example still sticks with me today in terms of why I succeeded, and why I was able to be great—because of Hacksaw and one marking pencil."

Bobb McKittrick

The unsung heroes of the 49ers through the years were the offensive linemen. Rarely did the 49ers spend high draft picks on offensive linemen, so the responsibility fell onto the shoul-

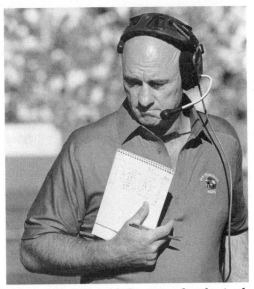

The late Bobb McKittrick molded groups of undersized players into some of the best offensive lines in football. (Photo by Brad Mangin)

ders of offensive line coach Bobb McKittrick to mold these generally undersized athletes into an important part of our success.

Bobb, a former Marine Corps officer, was quite a character. He was among Coach Bill Walsh's first hires in 1979. His toughness was one of his most memorable traits. He wanted his linemen to know how tough he was, so he'd go to our games in freezing weather wearing just a short-sleeved T-shirt.

In 1983, Bobb did not wear a jacket on the sideline at Soldier Field during a game played in freezing rain. He was so cold his teeth were chattering and he couldn't even communicate with his offensive linemen or the coaches on the headsets.

A few years later, when the 49ers played in subzero conditions again at Soldier Field for the NFC championship game, Coach Walsh ordered Bobb to wear a jacket. He had to order him to wear a jacket, because Bobb would undoubtedly have tried to go onto the field with short sleeves again.

Dying Without an Enemy

During his time, Bobb McKittrick came under scrutiny because of some of the blocking techniques he taught his offensive linemen. Defensive players did not take kindly to being cut-blocked or leg-whipped.

After a game against the Los Angeles Raiders in 1985, defensive lineman Howie Long followed Bobb off the field after he became incensed at some of the blocking techniques used against him. "I wish you'd put a helmet on so we could go at it," Howie reportedly told Bobb.

Nearly 15 years later when Bobb knew he was dying of cancer, he spoke with Joe Montana and told him he would like to have an opportunity to speak with Howie to clear the air. Joe relayed the message for Bobb.

"I called Bobb that night," Howie said. "It made me feel good to talk to him, and from what I could tell, it made him feel good, too. The biggest compliment I can give him is that I hope I'm one-tenth as courageous as Bobb was when I'm faced with my own mortality."

The Rev. Pat Richey, the 49ers' team chaplain at the time, said Bobb felt at peace with the way he left things with Howie. "Bobb told me that they had a great conversation and they only talked a little bit about the incident. It meant a lot to him."

Howie said his problems with Bobb were a distant memory. He said he did not hold any personal bitterness toward Bobb even before the two men spoke.

"I expressed my respect for him as a person and as a coach," Howie said. "I wanted him to know that I had no animosity. I was touched that he wanted to speak with me. We talked very little about football. We talked about our kids. I have three of my own, and he talked about his kids a little. We talked about life. He was very congratulatory of my being inducted into the Hall of Fame. I thanked him for that."

About a month after that conversation, in March 2000, Bobb McKittrick died after a 14-month battle with bile duct cancer. He was 64.

Dedicated to His Work

While Bobb McKittrick was going through his health problems, he received word in May 1999 he had been selected to undergo a liver transplant. How did he celebrate this news? He drove to the 49ers' facility to work with young offensive linemen Jeremy Newberry and Tyrone Hopson before going to the hospital.

But because the cancer had spread, the transplant could not be performed. Ten days later, Bobb was back on the practice field for an off-season mini-camp. Early that season, Bobb was honored at halftime of a 49ers game, and he knew full well what it meant.

"I'm not so naïve to think I would be up here if it weren't for what I'm going through," he told the crowd at Candlestick Park. "Assistant coaches don't usually get these kinds of awards."

Bobb McKittrick's legacy continues with the 49ers. Each season, the members of that close-knit fraternity vote the winner of the McKittrick Award, given to the team's best offensive lineman.

Bill McPherson

Bill McPherson joined Bill Walsh's first coaching staff in 1979, and he has been with the organization ever since.

Mac coached the linebackers and defensive line; he was the defensive coordinator, assistant head coach, general defensive assistant, personnel assistant, and now, he's a personnel consultant.

He helped keep our defenses together through the years. He and George Seifert worked very well together. He would come to work wearing cowboy boots, and he was ready to rock and roll.

I remember one training camp, he was riding a scooter around the Sierra College campus at night when he ran into a cable that was designed to keep people off the grass. He fell off that thing and broke his shoulder. He did not miss a day of practice. Although he was in intense pain, and deep down the players felt badly for him, we found his predicament an endless source of amusement.

It was easy to kid Coach Mac about his condition because everybody felt comfortable around him. He was a players' coach, for sure.

Paul Hackett and Dennis Green

The Bill Walsh coaching tree is amazing. Coach Walsh hired great coaches, and working on his staff made those coaches even better prepared to move on to other jobs and succeed.

When I first got to the 49ers, Paul Hackett was the offensive coordinator. He was instrumental in helping develop Joe Montana into the player he would become. Coach Hackett also deserves a lot of credit for working with me during my early days with the team.

He passed the torch on to Dennis Green, who worked with receivers for several seasons. Coach Green came in and did a real good job. He took what he learned from Coach Walsh and applied it to head coaching jobs at Northwestern and Stanford.

Coach Green later did a wonderful with the Minnesota Vikings, and now he's back in the league with the Arizona Cardinals. That is not good news to the 49ers, because the Cardinals are also in the NFC West. The Cardinals are not going to be the pushovers they've been in the past with Coach Green running the show.

He is a players' coach. Of course, he is still using the same philosophy that brought Coach Walsh so much success. He'll get the Cardinals running the West Coast offense as well as any team in the league in a short period of time.

Ray Rhodes

Ray Rhodes was the funniest coach I've met in my life. He used to play the game, and he still acted like a player even as a coach. He hung out with players to a certain extent, and he always talked a lot of trash.

He certainly got the most out of his defensive backs. He got all those guys in the secondary working well together, and they always played extremely hard. Coach Rhodes was the kind of guy who could motivate you to run through a brick wall for him.

As a defensive backs coach in 1981, Coach Rhodes got that young defensive backfield to play like veterans in almost no time. That was a testament to his coaching.

When he returned to the 49ers in 1994 as the defensive coordinator, it turned out to be just a one-year stint. He was hired the next season by the Philadelphia Eagles, and he promptly won NFL Coach of the Year. He also had a one-year stint as head coach of the Green Bay Packers and now is defensive coordinator under Mike Holmgrem with the Seattle Seahawks—another NFC West team.

Freddie Solomon

Freddie Solomon was a small-college quarterback at Tampa before joining the 49ers in 1978. Coach Walsh saw a lot of athletic ability and moved him to wide receiver, where he put together an outstanding eight-year career with the 49ers.

Freddie threw a nice ball, and there were times when we were running short on quarterbacks that he would step in there and take a few snaps. One year, during the playoffs, Coach Walsh devised a play in which Freddie would go in at quarterback and run the option.

He was a tremendous athlete, and he was also a bit of a mystery man. Nobody knew his age or how fast he was. But I remember he was plenty fast.

One year when we were playing the Washington Redskins, Freddie caught a hitch and turned upfield. He was in a race with Redskins cornerback Darrell Green, who was a multiple winner of the NFL's Fastest Man award. Not only didn't Green catch Freddie, but Freddie pulled away from him to score the touchdown.

Nobody other than Joe Montana was a bigger prankster than Freddie. He was in charge of the swag board in the locker room. He would always find different cartoon characters and put a jersey number on them to coincide with a teammate he was taking some shots at. It was crazy stuff.

One year during training camp, Fred Dean put a frog in Freddie's bed. Freddie spent the rest of training camp plotting his revenge. On the final day of camp, Freddie broke in to Fred's room and tore it apart. He dumped everything onto the floor and covered the entire room with baby powder. He might have even performed a bodily function in Fred's room, but don't tell anyone you heard it from me.

John Taylor, J.T., stayed out of the spotlight, but he was an integral part of our offense's success. (Photo by Brad Mangin)

John Taylor

With Jerry Rice and John Taylor, the 49ers had the best receiving tandem in the NFL for a long time.

J.T. did not get a whole lot of attention because he stopped talking to the media early in his career after having an issue about something personal that was written about him in the newspaper.

He was a tremendous athlete. He was so raw, he could've done many different things. He had the speed and strength to turn the short passes into long gains, just like Jerry. In fact, I think if J.T. had been the focus of the team's offense, he could have put up some of those numbers Jerry achieved.

J.T. was also a dangerous punt returner. In 1988, he returned two punts for touchdowns and had an impressive 12.6-yard average. Every time he touched the ball, you had the feeling something big was going to happen. It was like watching sandlot football. It seemed as if everyone else was in slow motion.

He was a complete player, too. He took a lot of pride in his blocking ability, which is something that has always set 49ers receivers apart from the rest. The public might not know it because he rarely conducted interviews, but J.T. was the nicest guy you'd ever want to meet. He retired after the 1995 season to devote all his energy to his trucking business on the East Coast.

Wendell Tyler

I am very fortunate the 49ers acquired Wendell Tyler in 1983. He helped get me ready for the NFL. It was a great idea to trade for a veteran guy who could help mentor a young draft pick until he was ready to take the job on his own.

For the first couple of seasons, I don't think Wendell was threatened by me. He was the halfback and I was the fullback. I was not a threat to rush for 1,000 yards in my first couple seasons in the league because I was more of a pass catcher.

Wendell rushed for 1,262 yards and seven touchdowns in 1984. But I knew my role was going to change the next year, after I scored three touchdowns in the Super Bowl. My third year is when I turned it on and showed I could put up big numbers in the league.

Wendell got banged up that next season, and that's when I had my 1,000 rushing-1,000 receiving achievement. Wendell never said anything, but I could tell he was a little hurt the young guy was taking over. I could sense he was a little envious. He knew his career was winding down, but at the same time he was happy for me.

Wendell certainly taught me well. I learned a lot from him about how to be a running back in the NFL.

Tom Rathman

When I was a senior at Nebraska, Tom Rathman was a redshirt freshman. When Tom came to the 49ers in 1986, I started seeing some time at halfback. Coach Walsh envisioned Tom becoming the fullback and blocking for me.

Tom Rathman, who came to the 49ers from Nebraska, was like a coach on the field. Now, he is a coach.(Photo by Brad Mangin)

I mentored Tom when he came to the 49ers. We studied together and I threw him a lot of passes so he would be prepared to be a receiver out of the backfield, which was a requirement for any 49ers back.

Tom was a crushing blocker who enjoyed going up against linebackers. Coach Walsh made him lose some weight—from about 245 to 230—when he came to the 49ers, but Tom didn't lose that stomach.

Joe Montana gave him the name "Woody," after the small-town country kid on "Cheers." But Tom was very sophisticated when it came to the game of football. Later in his career, he'd start coaching the offensive line and telling them what to do during games. He would even make the different gap calls. You could tell he would become a coach.

Tom coached 49ers running backs for seven seasons before moving on to the Detroit Lions with Steve Mariucci's staff in 2003.

Bill Ring

Bill Ring is a great success story, on and off the football field.

He went undrafted in 1979, but the Oakland Raiders signed him as a free agent. He lasted just three days with the Raiders until they decided after a spring mini-camp he was not good enough to make the team. So Bill went back to Brigham Young and earned his degree in finance while working as a graduate assistant on Coach Lavell Edwards' staff.

The next summer he went to camp with the Pittsburgh Steelers, and this time he made it to the next-to-last cut. He had a chance to play in the Canadian Football League, but his dream was to play in the NFL, so he did not take the invitation to play north of the border.

In 1981, he was invited to 49ers camp, and Coach Walsh liked what he saw and kept him on the roster. Several months later, Bill Ring was a key member of special teams and had a big seven-yard run to set up the 49ers' first touchdown in Super Bowl XVI against the Bengals.

Bill Ring was one of those guys who did whatever it took to help the team win. He was certainly an unsung hero. He was a scrappy player who worked his butt off and helped set the tone in practice. Linebackers knew they had to be concentrating during practice or he would take their heads off.

He wasn't the biggest or fastest guy on the field, but you could always count on him to rise to the occasion in the fourth quarter when guys on other teams started to tire. He won the prestigious Len Eshmont Award in 1983.

Bill spent six seasons in the NFL and has turned out to be even more successful in his post-football career. He has risen to the top of the field in investment banking, working as senior vice president at Capital Guardian Trust Company in San Francisco.

The 1983 Draft

The draft in which I was selected was pretty successful for the 49ers. In addition to my drafting in the second round, the team also got safety Tom Holmoe, linebacker Riki Ellison and offensive lineman Jesse Sapolu.

Holmoe did a great job for us as a nickelback for a lot of years. He was a very smart player and was never out of position. He worked hard and, of course, eventually became a coach at Stanford, then with the 49ers, and later as head coach at UC Berkeley.

Another player from that class would also become a coach. People might not remember, but Buffalo Bills coach Mike Mularkey was a ninth-round pick of the 49ers that year. He was a solid player, though he did not make the 49ers. He went on to play six seasons with the Minnesota Vikings.

But not everybody in that draft class worked as hard as the rest of us. Just a few picks after I was selected in the second round, we took linebacker Blanchard Montgomery of UCLA. He could've been a great linebacker, but he didn't have the focus and the discipline. He never came to camp in shape and was not willing to go the extra mile. He wanted to wear the uniform, but he didn't want to get it dirty. Montgomery spent only two seasons with the team. Gary Moten, who was taken in the seventh round, was another player with tons of potential who didn't take it seriously enough.

Carl Monroe

Carl Monroe came to the 49ers as an undrafted rookie. He was a good friend of mine, and he was my roommate on road trips during that first season. He was a small guy, but he snored like a grizzly bear.

I gave him the name "Money," because he was so versatile he could do anything. He was a running back but could play wide receiver, and he returned kickoffs and punts. He was a special guy.

Carl scored our first touchdown in Super Bowl XIX, when we beat the Miami Dolphins. Sadly, though, he died from cardiac arrest in 1989. He was 29. He was a mellow, down-to-earth guy who would do anything for his friends. I miss him a lot.

Jesse Sapolu

Today the NFL draft lasts only seven rounds. In 1983, the draft went 12 rounds, and offensive lineman Jesse Sapolu was selected in the 11th round. He played at Hawaii, and I don't think many people gave him a chance to succeed in the NFL.

Fortunately for Jesse, he was coached by Bobb McKittrick. Jesse had the work ethic and the willingness to incorporate everything Bobb taught him. He was a very coachable player, and he wanted to prove that a player selected in the 11th round could make it. Jesse played in the NFL at guard and center through the 1994 season, earning two trips to the Pro Bowl during his long career.

I roomed with Jesse during my first year in training camp, and it was just my luck Jesse snored like a sonic boom. Between Jesse and Carl Monroe, I never got any sleep during that first season with the 49ers.

Riki Ellison

I first met linebacker Riki Ellison at one of the combines prior to the draft. I remember Gil Brandt, the Dallas Cowboys' top personnel guy, did not exactly offer flattering evaluations of us.

He said I was injured too much and I would not be able to succeed in the NFL because I wasn't durable. He said Riki had bad knees and he'd be lucky to get drafted. I couldn't believe it when we ended up being drafted by the same team. We were happy to be teammates, and we both started as rookies.

The last game of our rookie year, we played the Dallas Cowboys on *Monday Night Football.* I rushed for two touchdowns in the game, and Riki was all over the field making tackles. On one play, he slammed down Tony Dorsett so hard it knocked the wind out of him.

We kicked their butts 42-17, and I remember us running off the field together laughing, "They said we couldn't play, huh?" Gil Brandt's comments from months earlier had served as great motivation to play against his team, that's for sure.

Riki and I became very good friends. I named my son, Rogdrick, partly after Riki. We called Rogdrick "Ricky" when he was little.

When I went to the Raiders later in my career, Riki had already made the move from the 49ers to the Raiders. We would drive together to our games at the Los Angeles Coliseum. Because Riki was a devoted alum of USC, he would always want to stop at the USC campus and meditate in front of the Trojan Horse statue on our way to games. It was a little bizarre and it wore on my patience, but he always made me take that detour.

Dwight Clark

Dwight Clark did not have that much talent, but he worked his ass off, was smart and ran precise pass patterns.

Of course, he supplied one of the great moments in team history when he made "The Catch" of that six-yard Joe Montana pass to win the 1981 NFC championship game over the Dallas Cowboys. That play was the seminal moment in team history and led the 49ers to their first Super Bowl.

And the fact it occurred is almost miraculous, because nobody had projected Dwight Clark as a future NFL player from his days at Clemson. Dwight had an unspectacular college career and only got his foot in the door because he picked up a phone call intended for his roommate.

In 1979, Coach Walsh went on a scouting trip to Clemson to take a look at a quarterback named Steve Fuller, who was

Dwight's roommate. When Coach Walsh called Fuller's room to set up a time to work out, Dwight answered the phone and introduced himself. Coach Walsh invited Dwight to tag along and catch passes for Fuller.

Coach Walsh liked what he saw from the tall, sure-handed receiver. The 49ers had traded away their first-round pick to the Buffalo Bills the previous year for O.J. Simpson, so Fuller was gone by the time they selected.

Instead, Coach Walsh waited until the third round to choose a quarterback from Notre Dame named Joe Montana.

But the trip to Clemson was not a complete waste, because Coach Walsh selected Dwight Clark in the 10th round. Of the nine players the 49ers selected that year after Montana, Dwight was the only one who played more than two seasons with the club.

Dwight always went out of his way to help me. He and Freddie Solomon would work with me on catching passes. He answered my every question and let me know everything I needed to know about playing in the NFL.

William "Bubba" Paris

Bubba was a dominating player in college at Michigan, but then he sustained a bad knee injury that limited his effectiveness in the pros. He still managed to be a solid player, despite having a bum knee.

The funny thing about Bubba is that everybody remembers him because of the problems he went through trying to keep his weight down. In those days, 300-pound offensive linemen were the exception. He was probably fined $300,000 in his career for being overweight.

The way I figure, they need to give him his money back. Now, look at all the players in the NFL who are 340 or more.

Bubba would be an average-sized offensive lineman by today's standards. It's sad everybody just remembers him for being overweight. Personally, I don't think it was that bad. I think he was so determined to lose weight that he was weak all the time. Plus, he had a difficult time keeping that weight off because it was tough for him to work out because of his knee.

John Ayers

John Ayers, the starting left guard through the 1986 season, was a hard worker and not afraid of anything. He used to drive people off the ball and knock them 10 yards down field until the whistle blew.

John and I had lockers next to each other, so we got to know each other very well. He loved to go pheasant hunting, and he'd always try to get me to go. I'd never go, but he'd always tell me, "Catfish, I'll bring back eight for you." He would marinate the pheasant in beer and smoke them for me. They tasted great.

It is really sad, but John died of liver cancer in 1995. He was a good ol' boy who did not have a lot to say, but he would give you the shirt off his back. We had a strong mutual respect.

Fred Quillan

Fred Quillan was a damn good center with the 49ers. He already had put together some good years with the team when I came to the 49ers. He twice made the Pro Bowl team, but in 1985, he got injured in the game and was never quite the same after that.

He was the second quarterback of the offense. Of course, there was Joe Montana who made all the plays that everybody noticed. But Fred made all the line calls, so he had to know the offense inside and out. It was his responsibility to make sure everybody on the offensive line was on the same page. He was also the long snapper and performed that job very well for many years.

Randy Cross

A lot of people know Randy Cross as one of the best football analysts on television, but he was also an outstanding player for the 49ers during his career.

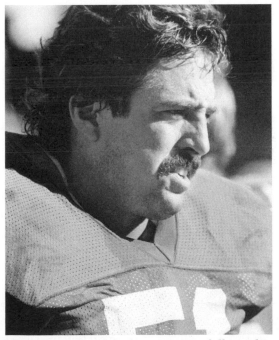

Randy Cross was so fast, I had to get up to full speed in a hurry when he was leading a sweep or he'd outrun me. (Photo by Brad Mangin)

He was the first pick of the 49ers in the 1976 draft. Randy suffered through some lean years with the 49ers until everything turned around in 1981.

He started 12 games as a rookie at center and played there until he moved to guard in 1978. When Bobb McKittrick came on the scene in 1979, that's when Randy's career really took off. Randy moved back to center to finish his career after Fred Quillan messed up his knee.

Randy was just as quick as a lot of running backs, so I had to make sure I was ready to run at full speed any time a play called for him to lead a sweep for me. We used to run "38 Sweep," and Randy would pull and come around the edge. I'd get on his hip and he'd pull me around the corner. He would just crush cornerbacks, and I would always get big yardage.

When the 49ers won the Super Bowl in 1981, Randy was selected to his first Pro Bowl. He went on to make three trips to Hawaii for the game.

Keith Fahnhorst

Keith Fahnhorst was a solid player at right tackle, and he also helped keep the team together in the locker room. He was the team spokesman. Any time there was a problem and there were guys who were unhappy about something, Keith was the guy to deal with the crisis and keep us going.

Keith played almost his entire career with the 49ers with the knowledge that he had a kidney condition that would need to be addressed in the years after his career was over. In 1976, running back Delvin Williams hit him from behind. Keith's kidney was punctured, and doctors told him it would heal on its own. But then a bunch of cysts were discovered on his kidney, and he was diagnosed with polycystic kidney disease. The disease can go unnoticed for years, so it was actually fortunate he got injured in that practice.

Because the disease is genetic, a family donor was not an option. But Keith got extremely lucky when a virtual stranger who attended the same Bible study group in Minnesota came forward to volunteer one of his kidneys. The man had been in the United States just 10 years after emigrating from Nigeria. Keith was flabbergasted someone would make such a huge sacrifice for him. The successful transplant surgery took place in February 2003.

Keith told me what this man had done for him, so I called him to express my appreciation for what he had done for one of my teammates. I sent him an autographed football and an autographed photo. Things are going very well for Keith. When the 49ers played the Vikings in 2003 in Minneapolis, Keith was able to attend the game and meet the team beforehand.

Harris Burton and Steve Wallace

I played with Harris Barton and Steve Wallace, but they later really came into their own as bookend offensive tackles after I left the 49ers. In fact, they were such a large part of the team's offensive success that they later signed identical contracts because of their equal importance to the team.

Some people stress out before games. Heck, I had trouble sleeping. But nobody was ever as bad as Harris. This guy needed some serious calm-down pills.

He was such a nervous wreck he made everybody around him nervous and uptight, too. He would drive you crazy in the locker room because he'd be pacing the floor and talking to himself. Then he would start working on his technique while making grunting noises.

Harris nearly worried himself to death. The funny thing is he didn't have anything to worry about. He was a great player. He came from North Carolina, where they ran the ball a lot. He was fast and could get out front and lead sweeps. He also became a really good pass protector, too. He took pride in learning his technique, and he adapted quickly to Coach McKittrick's way of doing things.

Harris was the 49ers' first-round draft pick in 1987. Because of Coach McKittrick's skill at developing unheralded offensive linemen, the 49ers did not draft another offensive lineman in the first round until taking Kwame Harris with the first pick in 2003.

He started Super Bowls at right tackle and right guard. Harris Barton made the Pro Bowl only one time in his career, but in six different seasons he received some All-Pro recognition. I just wish he could have enjoyed it a little more.

Steve Wallace was a fourth-round draft pick in 1986. He started 16 games at left tackle in 1988, then was moved to right tackle in 1990. From '91 to '96, he was back to left tackle, making the Pro Bowl once during that time. We called Steve Wallace "Big Sexy" because he was a great dresser and had debonair ways.

Guy McIntyre

Players today all want to do their own thing and capture the individual glory. Coach Walsh's mentality was to instill the big picture in all of us.

That's why he could go get a guy like Guy McIntyre, who weighed just 271 pounds when he was drafted out of Georgia in 1984. In reality, Guy was somewhere between a guard and a tight end. Coach Walsh liked him because he was explosive and could attack the linebacker head-on.

So before Guy became one of the stalwarts on the offensive line, Coach Walsh would put him onto the field at fullback in short-yardage and goal-line situations. We called the formation "Angus."

Guy came in once when we played the Chicago Bears, and he drilled middle linebacker Mike Singletary, allowing us to run right down their throats with Wendell Tyler. That move inspired Chicago Bears coach Mike Ditka to use William "Refrigerator" Perry in the same role throughout the 1984 season.

The "Fridge" became a national hero because of his role on offense. So the "Fridge" can thank Guy McIntyre for helping get him all that money he made in endorsements.

Fred Dean

Early in the 1981 season, Coach Walsh found the missing piece to the puzzle. His name was Fred Dean, and the 49ers acquired him for a couple draft picks. Less than a week after arriving in a trade, Fred was starting and playing a major role in the 49ers' big victory over the Dallas Cowboys that gave the team the confidence that carried them to the Super Bowl title.

In that first game, Dean recorded three sacks and two quarterback hurries and batted down two passes in the 49ers' 45-14 win over the Cowboys. "We didn't know it at the time, but he turned it around," Coach Walsh said. "It all started in that first game. He did things that shocked everybody."

Fred won NFL Defensive Player of the Year in his first season with the 49ers, and in 1983 he recorded 17 1/2 sacks, including a then NFL record six in a victory over the New Orleans Saints.

There is no doubt in my mind Fred Dean should be in the Hall of Fame. He was a dominant pass rusher during his days.

He was amazing because he weighed only 235 pounds soaking wet.

Moreover, he never lifted a weight in his life. He once said whenever he felt as if he should have been lifting weights, he would lie down until the urge passed. Fred didn't take particularly good care of his body. He was also a chain smoker.

In those days, it was not out of the ordinary to see players puffing cigarettes in their down time. I would look around and see Fred, Dwight Hick, Freddie Solomon and Lawrence Pillars all smoking cigarettes and wonder how they managed to play at such a high level. Fred probably did not maximize all of his potential as a player, but that does not diminish the fact he was still an incredible performer.

He might not have lifted weights, but he was as naturally strong as anybody who worked out eight hours a day. I remember watching him on ESPN on one of those NFL arm-wrestling matches. He'd easily beat guys who outweighed him by 100 pounds.

Fred also battled migraine headaches throughout most of his career. In 1976, he ran head first into a TV camera stand on the sideline, and he started having regular headaches shortly thereafter. His migraines have gotten worst since his retirement.

Fred was quite a character. When he played in San Diego, he was in a singing group with Kellen Winslow and John Jefferson. Fred is a good singer, and he was also a cook. He would always have some of us over to his house for Thanksgiving dinner.

Dwaine Board

When I came to the team, Dwaine Board had hurt his knee and slowed down a bit. But he was still a valuable member of the team, as George Seifert liked to use a rotation of different players on the defensive line to keep everybody fresh.

We had guys like Board, Jim Stuckey, Lawrence Pillars, Manu Tuiasosopo, Jeff Stover, Michael Carter, Pete Kugler and John Harty, who all fit a role and were very unselfish players.

Dwaine was a smart guy. He became an assistant coach with the 49ers in 1990 and remained with the team until Dennis Erickson was hired in 2003. Dwaine is now the defensive line coach with the Seattle Seahawks.

Russ Francis

If Russ Francis was told he could not ride a motorcycle, he would come riding up on the loudest chopper he could find. If he was told that he could not fly airplanes, he would make sure he had an open-cockpit plane. Russ was the maverick of our team.

He would always ask me to go up in the plane with him, and I always said no. I knew if he got me up there, he would be doing all kinds of double-loops trying to make me sick.

I love Russ. He's a great guy. He's a daredevil and quite adventurous. He parachutes and is an accomplished skier. He isn't afraid of anything.

Everybody remembers Russ was a great receiver, but he was also one heck of a blocker. He did a great job, but he always gave Coach Walsh a hard time. Those two were always going at it.

Russ made the Pro Bowl three times while with the New England Patriots. Coach Walsh traded first- and fourth-round picks for him in 1982, and he played a significant role on the 1984 Super Bowl team.

John Frank

It's not often a professional football player walks away from a lucrative and promising future in the sport to pursue a career in another field. That is why everybody was surprised when tight end John Frank decided to return to medical school after the 1988 season.

John was fearless on the football field. I never saw him afraid of anything. He body-slammed Lawrence Taylor, and that pretty much wrapped up a spot on the All-Madden Team for him that season.

John was a second-round draft pick from Ohio State. He was prepared to retire after the 1987 season, after splitting time with Russ Francis. But John's mother convinced him to play one more season. He is glad he took his mom's advice, because we won the Super Bowl that year.

He retired at the age of 27, earned his M.D. from Ohio State in 1992 and spent six years in residency in Chicago. Now he is a successful cosmetic surgeon in San Francisco. And he does not regret his decision to take his career in a different direction.

Brent Jones

Brent Jones took advantage of John Frank's sudden retirement to carve a very good career for himself. I don't think Brent would have played that much if John had stayed around.

Brent had been cut by the Pittsburgh Steelers, but he found his niche with the 49ers. He and Steve Young were best friends, so they developed a great rapport on the field. Brent had great hands, but his speed was suspect. So Brent took it upon himself to work with a speed coach.

All Brent wanted to do was catch the football, and he did that very well. He caught 417 passes in his career with the 49ers and was a huge part of the team's success with the downfield passing game. But Brent did not focus that much on blocking, and I paid the price for it. I remember getting crushed by a line-backer and wondering what the heck just happened. Then I'd find out that Brent missed a block.

Jamie Williams

Can you imagine making it to the NFL and then several years later having one of your best childhood friends become a team-mate? That's what happened to me when the 49ers signed tight end Jamie Williams as a Plan B free agent in 1989.

Bill Walsh came to me to ask if we should sign Jamie, and before he even finished his question, I said, "Yes, get him!" He was the most dominating blocker I had ever seen.

Jamie and I grew up together in Davenport, Iowa, and although he was one year ahead of me, we played together on the same elementary school, junior high, high school and col-lege teams. He went to Nebraska and redshirted as a freshman. I went there a year later and played as a freshman. We were roommates at Nebraska for four years.

Jamie placed a lot of emphasis on his blocking, and it showed. Our junior high coach, Lou Williams, was an All-Big Ten player at Iowa, and he spent some time with the Green Bay Packers under Vince Lombardi.

Coach Williams was a mentor to a lot of kids in Davenport, and he earned our respect. He molded Jamie mentally into a tough blocker and showed him the proper technique to get the job done. Jamie could fire out and punch a defender in the chest and completely knock him off the line of scrimmage. Jamie learned how to do it properly at an early age, and it carried over to every level of football he played for the remainder of his career.

It was always a pleasure to get my number called and know I'd be running behind my old friend Jamie Williams.

Chapter 4

THE SUPER BOWLS

Football is the ultimate team game. A player can get all kinds of individual accomplishments, but the one honor everyone strives for is to be crowned a Super Bowl champion.

Probably the proudest accomplishment of my 11-year NFL career is that I never once sat at home to see others out there competing in the playoffs. I started eight seasons with the 49ers, and during that time we won three Super Bowls.

Sometimes people will ask what it would have been like to lose one of those Super Bowls. I'm just glad I never found out. Most players work so hard to get to that stage in the season, and once you make it to that final game, winning becomes all the more important.

Is it a lost season if you lose in the Super Bowl? Heck, no. But I would imagine it leaves you with a sense of unfinished business.

The San Francisco 49ers of the 1980s were all about business. We never viewed a trip to Miami or New Orleans for the Super Bowl as a vacation. South Beach and Bourbon Street might be where the fun was, but we knew if we took care of our business and won the football game, the fun that would follow would be enough to last a lifetime.

Sure, we had fun along the journey. Sometimes we didn't have as much fun as other teams might have enjoyed because we were so focused on the job at hand. Looking back on it, we handled the obligations perfectly.

The Super Bowl is the most watched sporting event in the United States. Even people who don't know or care all that much about football will plop down on the couch to watch the game.

Every player wants to shine brightest in the Super Bowl. There were many outstanding individual performances in those victories, but in the three Super Bowls in which I played, we put together outstanding team performances. We shone collectively, as a team. And that's the way I'll remember those Super Bowls—as the culmination of three tremendous teams coming together at exactly the right time.

The Ring Is the Thing

I have three Super Bowls rings, but you won't see me wearing them around town.

My Super Bowl rings are in a safe-deposit box in Redwood City, where they will remain for the foreseeable future. As far as I'm concerned, a Super Bowl ring is like a trophy. And there is no reason to go around showcasing your awards.

If somebody wins an Olympic gold medal, you wouldn't expect that person to go around wearing it around his neck, would you?

I have willed my Super Bowl rings to my children. Hopefully, those rings will be family heirlooms, passed down from generation to generation as a lasting symbol of the commitment those 49ers teams made to each other.

People in my office at TIBCO Software are always asking me why I don't bring in my rings so they can see them. Maybe I will some day, but I haven't gotten my rings out of that safe-deposit box since the day I put them in there.

You hear stories about athletes who had to sell their Super Bowl rings because of hardships they endured later in life. That breaks my heart to know somebody worked his whole career and lived the dream of winning a Super Bowl and then had to sell his treasure because life became too difficult.

In the ultimate team sport, I could not have been happier to have Joe Montana as my quarterback. We won three Super Bowls together. (Photo by Brad Mangin)

Super Bowl XIX

A lot of players go their entire careers without tasting what it's like to play in a Super Bowl. I was lucky enough to find myself playing in the big game in my second year in the league.

On January 20, 1985, the 49ers proved we were not going to be just a one-hit wonder with a 38-16 victory over the Miami Dolphins in Super Bowl XIX.

Just three years earlier, the 49ers won Super Bowl XVI over the Cincinnati Bengals at the Pontiac Silverdome. But the organization had a difficult time keeping momentum going because the 1982 season was marred by the strike, and they finished with a 3-6 record.

The following year, my rookie season, we had a great team, but we lost to the Washington Redskins in the NFC championship game because of a couple of phantom pass-interference calls on our secondary in the final minutes.

That was a tough one to swallow. We felt like we were the better team. I still feel like we were the better team, but the Redskins took advantage of some generous calls to win the game 24-21 and advance to the Super Bowl.

We all made a pact to come back and win the Super Bowl the next year. Coach Bill Walsh was pissed after that game. Heck, we all were pissed.

In the '84 season, we showed the resilience and determination to get back to the NFC championship game after posting a 15-1 record in the regular season. This time, we left no doubt, as our defense recorded nine sacks and allowed the Bears just 186 yards of total offense for a 23-0 victory at Candlestick Park.

With that victory, our ticket was punched to the Super Bowl. It was the 49ers' second trip to the Super Bowl in franchise history and my first.

Getting into the Right Mindset

"Hacksaw" Reynolds was a grizzled veteran. He knew the significance of making it to the Super Bowl, and he made sure the younger players fully appreciated the grandeur of the event. Hacksaw came up to me one day leading up to the game and said, "Play your heart out, because you never know if you'll have an opportunity to come back here."

I took those words to heart. I wasn't about to get caught up in all the outside stuff that can affect your performance. I tried not to worry about all the media attention or stress out over getting tickets for my family.

One thing I prided myself on was being a good listener. I paid attention to guys like Hacksaw, Fred Dean and Gary "Big Hands" Johnson. I tried to conduct myself in a very professional manner, just like the veteran leaders of that team.

I was so focused on everything Coach Walsh was saying the entire two weeks. I didn't want to have anything else come into my thoughts. I was concentrating so hard on everything he said, I was looking right through him. I remembered every word that came out of his mouth.

Ready to Play

I always had a tough time sleeping before big games. This went all the way back to my high school days. I enjoyed competing, and just thinking about playing in a game was enough to get my juices flowing. Obviously, a rush of adrenaline is not exactly conducive to a good night of sleep.

Jamie Williams was my teammate in junior high, high school, college and for two seasons with the 49ers. We roomed together when our high school team went to Cedar Falls for the Iowa state championship game.

This is what he had to say about my restlessness the night before games:

"Roger is so hyperactive, such a prankster, that it was tough to get any sleep. The day of the game, he'd wake up at 6 a.m., take a shower, then dive onto my bed, trying to wrestle me to the floor. Or we'd stay up until two in the morning and, after I finally go to sleep, he'd whisper in my ear: 'Jamie … Jamie. Get up. I can't sleep. I've got to talk to somebody.' Sometimes he'd knock on people's doors in the middle of the night and tackle them when they came out in the hall."

Well, I can neither confirm nor deny those stories, but you can imagine how excited I was to play in my first Super Bowl. My roommate was Ronnie Lott. This is what he had to say about the experience of being stuck with me:

"The night before Super Bowl XIX we were lying quietly on our beds watching the late-night news, and there were some Miami fans on TV rooting for the Dolphins. Suddenly, Roger jumped out of bed, ran over to the screen and started yelling, 'We're going to kick your butts! We're going to kick your butts!' Then he ran over to my bed and gave me a high five. He must have given me 10 straight high fives before we went to bed that night."

Breakout Game

I had a good year as a rookie, but I was by no means a nationally known player. Certainly fans of the 49ers knew all about me, but I had not yet broken through on the national stage.

As a rookie, I caught 48 passes and rushed for 725 yards and led the team with 12 touchdowns, but I finished second in the Rookie of the Year voting to Eric Dickerson of the L.A. Rams. Remember, I was a fullback. My main job was still to block for halfback Wendell Tyler.

My second year, Wendell rushed for 1,262 yards. I took tremendous pride in that accomplishment. I was never concerned about getting a lot of carries; I knew the best way for me to help the team was to block for Wendell, and that's what I did.

During the Super Bowl pregame show on ABC, O.J. Simpson came on TV and said, "Watch out for Roger Craig. He's going to be the unsung hero of the game."

I had not talked to O.J. and I did not know he said that until I watched a tape of the game. Well, O.J. was right.

We were trailing 10-7 in the second quarter when I caught an eight-yard touchdown pass from Joe Montana. Before the end of the half, I had a two-yard scoring run to give us a 28-16 lead.

In the third quarter, I caught a 16-yard TD pass from Joe. We won 38-16, and I set a Super Bowl record with three touchdowns. I had 58 yards rushing on 15 carries and caught seven passes for 77 yards.

A few weeks later, I thanked O.J. for his kind words about me. The following year, he asked me to have a role on his show, *First and Ten*, a series that aired on HBO.

Home-Crowd Edge

One of the great things about Super Bowl XIX was it was held at Stanford Stadium, in nearby Palo Alto. It was the closest thing to playing a home game without actually being in Candlestick Park.

We were able to continue practicing at our facility, which was located in Redwood City. There was no traveling, and we could pretty much keep to our routine. The game was being held in our back yard, and ticket scalpers were fetching more than $1,000 for tickets because of the excitement generated from having a local team in the game.

I'll always remember when my name was announced before the game and I ran out in front of 84,059 screaming fans. I had goose bumps on my body that were so big, I thought they were going to explode. I was floating on air.

I had to keep telling myself to relax and to focus on what the older guys had taught me. That was the most intense game

I ever played in my life. When I later watched the film of the game, I could tell I ran every play with vengeance, attitude, urgency and intensity.

There was one play when we had a short-yardage situation and Guy McIntyre was in the backfield. They put me at tailback because I was good at jumping over the pile. When I jumped, I was hit three times in the air and was spinning every which way. Fortunately, I got the first down to keep the drive alive. That play showed the determination of both teams.

It was great to be playing in a game so close to home. I knew we had the Dolphins where we wanted them when the fog starting to roll in over the top of Stanford Stadium.

Marino Mania

Coming into that game, everybody was talking about the Miami Dolphins and Dan Marino. In 1984, Marino had an unbelievable season. He threw 48 touchdown passes and had more than 5,000 yards passing.

People seemed to forget our offense was pretty good, and we had a quarterback who wasn't too shabby, either. Plus, our determined defense had a little something to prove, too.

We took the attitude that we wanted to show the world our offense was better than the Dolphins'. And our defense wanted to show the world it wasn't just going to roll over and let Marino have his way.

I think we proved our point. We rolled up 537 yards of offense, shattering the old Super Bowl record of the Oakland Raiders by 108 yards. We outgained the Dolphins by 223 yards.

It was definitely an "Us Against the World" mentality. All the experts had picked us to lose. Here's Joe and Dan Marino. They're both from Western Pennsylvania, and Joe did not want the young kid to show him up.

Our defensive backfield was outstanding. Carlton Williamson and Eric Wright both had interceptions. And all those guys back there, including Ronnie Lott and Dwight Hicks, were determined to dish out some hot licks every time a Dolphins receiver saw a pass come his way.

Time to Celebrate

Even though we were just a few minutes from our homes, we were locked into a hotel for the week leading up to the Super Bowl. After the win, I didn't even go to the celebration party.

I was so happy I rented a limousine and took my wife, Vernessia, for a night in San Francisco. We had a great dinner at an Italian restaurant on Fishermen's Wharf. The city was crazy that night. People were going nuts over the Super Bowl.

Suddenly I had become a star, and I wasn't accustomed to that kind of treatment. People were running up to the limo and celebrating with us. It was kind of dangerous, but it was also a lot of fun.

Cover Boy

A couple days after the game, I was heading back to Davenport to visit my family and friends when somebody on my flight said, "Did you see *Sports Illustrated*? You're on the cover."

When the flight landed, I went to the nearest newsstand and there it was. I was floored. There I am, high-stepping it into the end zone past diving Dolphins safety Mike Kozlowski. The cover reads, "Roger Craig Hammers the Dolphins."

In my hometown people were wearing buttons in honor of me. That was a great feeling to know the people of Davenport fully supported me.

Return on Investment

It was my second year in the league, and I did not have a shoe contract. The week of the Super Bowl, Mizuno approached me about wearing their shoe in the game. Most of the other big-name players had their own shoe contracts, so nobody wanted to wear Mizuno.

I agreed to wear the shoe for $3,000. I really didn't know anything about the Mizuno, other than that it was a Japanese-based company.

Mizuno got a pretty good return on their investment. Not only did I have a great game, but my picture—and their shoe—was on the cover of *Sports Illustrated*. I later signed a contract with them, and I wore the shoe for the remainder of my career. I had a hand in designing a shoe to better fit my needs, and they later signed Montana, John Elway and Steve Young to shoe deals.

Super Bowl XXIII

Our road to the Super Bowl in the 1988 season was difficult at times.

In mid-November we lost back-to-back games at Phoenix and at home against the Los Angeles Raiders to drop to 6-5. The Super Bowl was the last thing on our minds. We were just trying to make the playoffs.

But we got hot at the right time to win the NFC West. Our crowning achievement came when we beat the Bears in freezing conditions at Soldier Field in the NFC championship game. We then took care of business against the Bengals with a thrilling 20-16 victory to win Super Bowl XXIII.

No Time to Panic

Our last-second victory over the Bengals in Miami displayed the West Coast offense at its best. The final drive demonstrated everything we stood for as a team. Everybody was unselfish and everybody understood his role.

Montana, of course, was the leader. And everybody else had to follow the plan for us to be successful.

Even though we were down by three points with 3:20 remaining and backed up to our own eight-yard line, we still felt very much in control. During the TV timeout before we began "The Drive," Joe was joking in the huddle. I remember him saying, "Hey, look over there, it's John Candy."

Sure enough, there was John Candy in the stands. We were relaxed and loose, and there was no doubt the Bengals were on their heels.

Once it got down to business, Joe took over. He orchestrated our offense all the way down the field. He kept reminding everybody to get as many yards as we could, but to protect the ball and get out of bounds when we had a chance.

In many ways, the two-minute offense was our comfort zone. We rehearsed the drill in practice every week. But, more than that, we probably used the offense in games more than any other team in the league.

We often used the offense in the closing moments of the first half of games to tack on a touchdown or a field goal before heading into the locker room. Of course, it was always great to get points before halftime, but it was also important for getting us into the right frame of mind to move the ball without a huddle when we would need to do it at the end of a game.

Starting in a Hole

Our entire season—and that of the Bengals—all came down to one drive. There was no room for error, but we made one when we received the kickoff after Jim Breech's 40-yard field goal gave Cincinnati a 16-13 lead.

We started on our own eight-yard line after a holding penalty on the kickoff. The first play was critical to get out of this hole we had dug for ourselves. Joe tossed a short pass my way, and I gained eight yards on the play.

That was the strategy we took all the way down the field. Tight end John Frank caught a seven-yard pass, Jerry Rice had a seven-yard reception, and I gained four yards and a first down on a critical third-and-two play.

Now We're in Business

With a first down on our own 35, Joe Montana found Jerry Rice for a 17-yard gain on the left sideline. We had the Bengals worried now. Joe threw me a pass that I turned into a 13-yard gain for another first down.

After another penalty set us back 10 yards and made it second and 20, Joe and Jerry hooked up again. This time they connected for 27 yards and a first down to the 18-yard line.

Again, Joe looked my way on the next play. The pass was good for an eight-yard gain down to the 10-yard line with 39 seconds remaining.

Confusion on Touchdown

Everybody remembers that John Taylor caught the game-winning pass on a 10-yard throw from Joe with 34 seconds remaining. What people don't know is Tom Rathman and I almost blew it.

Because Tom and I communicated so well together, we would often switch positions on the field without anyone knowing it. We were pretty much interchangeable at halfback and fullback.

On the game-winning play —"20-Halfback Curl X-Up"— I was designated to be the primary option. I was supposed to run a curl route over the middle, and the plan was for Joe to dump it off to me. I should have lined up on the left side, but instead Tom and I mistakenly went to the wrong sides.

When Tom and I both realized we were in the wrong spots, we decided to just go ahead and run the play without switching sides. Because I was now the fullback, I should've stayed in the backfield to block.

But I knew I was supposed to be the intended target, so I released out of the backfield. And because Tom figured he had taken over my responsibility, he also ran a curl route on the other side. Because of the confusion, there was nobody left in the backfield to pick up the blitz.

The Bengals blitzed two linebackers on the play. I saw them coming at Joe out of the corner of my eye as I was leaving the backfield. As you can imagine, I was more than a little scared of what might happen.

Luckily, Joe saw the blitz coming and quickly went to John Taylor, his secondary receiver. Obviously, everything turned out all right, but it was one of those things that could have been disastrous.

Bad News Awaits

Our locker room was quite joyous after that victory. Everybody had to think that the 49ers were going to finally lose a Super Bowl, and we managed to pull it out with a pressure-packed final drive.

While I was celebrating with some teammates, broadcaster Brent Musburger was interviewing Coach Walsh on the podi-

Joe Montana makes a familiar signal after throwing a TD pass to Brent Jones in the first quarter of Super Bowl XXIV. (Photo by Brad Mangin)

um. He asked Coach Walsh if this were, indeed, his final game as coach of the 49ers. Coach Walsh began to cry.

It wasn't until later that evening I found out that Coach Walsh had retired as coach of the 49ers. I didn't know he was going to do that. He surprised all of us.

Coach Walsh understood me as a player better than any coach I'd ever had. He knew my strengths and my weaknesses, and he knew how to utilize my skills to best serve the team. When he retired, a part of me died. I wasn't the same running back after he stepped down as coach.

Of course, looking back on it, Coach Walsh stepped away too soon. He was still a great coach and he had a lot more years left in him. We won the Super Bowl the following year under George Seifert, but it wasn't George's team.

Only after Joe Montana left and Steve Young came in as the full-time starter did it truly become George's team.

As much as I wish Walsh had remained coach of the 49ers for my entire career with the organization, I fully understand his reason for leaving when he did. He basically got fed up with owner Eddie DeBartolo.

Coach Walsh had already won two Super Bowls with his players. His philosophy permeated throughout the building. But after the Minnesota Vikings upset us 36-24 in the 1987 NFC divisional playoff game, Eddie stripped Walsh of his president and general manager titles.

Coach Walsh had built the franchise from scratch, and he was basically stripped of his power because of one bad game. To me, that didn't make any sense at all.

That was Bill Walsh's team. The success of the franchise was due to Walsh's vision and Eddie's financial backing. But eventually Eddie wanted to bring in his own people. That is when Carmen Policy came into the picture. Eddie's father gave him the leeway to do his thing with the 49ers, and that's what Eddie did.

Super Bowl XXIV

From the time we reported to training camp for our first season under George Seifert, we were definitely on a mission to achieve back-to-back Super Bowl titles.

Our only losses the entire season came at home—a one-point setback to the Rams and a 21-17 defeat to the Green Bay Packers. But once we got into the playoffs, we steamrolled teams.

We beat the Vikings 41-13, then took care of the Rams 30-3 in the NFC championship game. Expecting a tough game from the Denver Broncos, we were surprised at how little resistance we ran up against in a 55-10 victory in Super Bowl XXIV in New Orleans.

Big Upset in the Big Easy?

We might have gone into the game as an 11 1/2-point favorite over the Broncos at the Louisiana Superdome, but something strange tends to happen during the two-week preparation period.

Because the media tend to run out of things to write about or talk about and everybody over-analyzes everything pertaining to a Super Bowl, invariably the underdog starts looking better to everyone.

So as the week in New Orleans wore on and on, we started hearing how the Broncos were working harder than we were. They were going through double-day practices. This was supposed to make them better prepared for this game than we were.

According to everything we heard, the 49ers were ripe for an upset.

Near the end of Super Bowl XXIV against the Broncos, Jerry Rice proclaims the 49ers to be No. 1 for the second consecutive season. (Photo by Brad Mangin)

We Were Upset, All Right

I was stunned. I think all of us were. Here we were at halftime of the Super Bowl and it was already a blowout.

For two weeks we heard the Denver Broncos talk a big game. They were saying how they were a physical team and we were a finesse team—yep, that old finesse label again. The

Broncos kept saying they were going to be aggressive against us and intimidate us.

With that in mind, we were expecting a physical game against the Broncos. We kept our mouths shut and just prepared mentally for the football game, while the Broncos were wearing themselves out with their long practices.

We were fresh and ready to go and we went up and down the field at will. We led 27-3 at halftime, and it wasn't even that close. I remember thinking, "This is going to be a pretty boring game if this continues." And it did continue. I wonder how many millions of people turned off their televisions.

You would think a 55-10 victory in the Super Bowl would be fun, but it wasn't. We were expecting a tense and tightly con-tested game, but it just never turned out that way.

Running Up the Score?

Later, I'd watch stuff on NFL Films about our Super Bowl win over the Broncos and their players were on the sideline talking about how we were trying to run up the score on them.

Heck, we weren't trying to run up the score. We just con-tinued to play football and the Broncos never stepped up and stopped us. It was just one of those games where everything went our way.

Jerry Rice was catching passes all over the field, and it seemed like everybody on our team scored. Jerry had three touchdowns, and Brent Jones, Tom Rathman, John Taylor and I all scored one apiece.

I can't even remember that much about the game because it just seemed like everything happened so easily. The Broncos really surprised me because they did not come to play. That was obvious.

Even a competitor like Matt Millen could not help but feel sorry for Broncos quarterback John Elway in our blowout victory in Super Bowl XXIV. (Photo by Brad Mangin)

Feeling Pity

Yep, this was not your ordinary game. Football players are supposed to get into the mindset of going for the jugular and finishing off the opponent.

Well, we did that all right against the Broncos. But even some of our most fierce competitors still could not help but feel sorry for the opponents. One player who comes to mind is linebacker Matt Millen.

When you watch the highlights of the game, you'll see Millen grab Broncos quarterback John Elway by the jersey as Elway is dejectedly leaving the field after another failed series.

"I felt sorry for Elway at one point," Millen said afterward. "Believe me, I haven't felt sorry for many quarterbacks."

Broncos Needed 49ers

The Broncos had a lot of the elements you need in a championship football team, but they were also lacking a lot. They had Bobby Humphrey at running back and a decent defense, but it wasn't until Terrell Davis came along to help take some of the heat off quarterback John Elway that the Broncos took it to another level.

They lost three Super Bowls with Elway at quarterback, and it also took some 49ers influence for them to break that slide.

After the 49ers won Super Bowl XXIX over the San Diego Chargers, the Broncos hired 49ers offensive coordinator Mike Shanahan. He brought former 49ers assistant Gary Kubiak with him to be his offensive coordinator.

When the Broncos finally won two Super Bowls in a row in the late 1990s, they had the West Coast offense embedded as their system. The Broncos took the 49ers' philosophy, and it worked for them, too.

Chapter 5

END OF AN ERA

Of course, I wish I could have remained with the 49ers for my entire career. But sometimes things happen that are out of your control.

I came to the 49ers as an unheralded rookie after a frustrating senior season at Nebraska. Coach Walsh and the 49ers trusted and believed in me, and I gave the organization everything I had for as many years as I was with the team.

My 49ers career ended after the 1990 season with a lot of tears and hurt feelings, but I certainly have no regrets about my football career. It was an amazing journey.

All events in a person's life shape who that person becomes. I've tried to use my own adversity as teaching tools for my children, who have all carved out niches in their own lives, on and off their respective playing fields.

Although I went on to play three more seasons in the NFL and never put on the 49ers uniform again, it meant a lot to me to retire as a member of the organization. I realize a lot of 49ers fans never truly accepted me with the Los Angeles Raiders or Minnesota Vikings.

While I'm truly grateful for the opportunities I was given with the Raiders and Vikings, I fully understand fans of the 49ers never viewed me as anything but a San Francisco 49er.

For that reason, I returned briefly to the organization in July of 1994 so I could officially retire as a member of the 49ers. And as much as I'd like to say I had something to do with it, I'm sorry I can't accept any credit for the 49ers' fifth Super Bowl title, which came to fruition that season.

I worked hard during my time with the 49ers. My obsession with fitness is the reason I sustained a high level of play throughout the 1980s, despite the inherent dangers of playing running back in the NFL.

Even today, I consider myself lucky to be in such good shape more than a decade after I last played football. To keep my competitive edge, I've started running marathons. A lot of players are so banged up after their careers are over they're living in constant pain, so I realize I am blessed to still be able to push my body to the limit.

Many of the friendships I forged with my teammates on those 49ers teams of the 1980s continue to this day. Unfortunately, I never experienced the same close relationship with former 49ers owner Eddie DeBartolo as I had before my final game with the 49ers.

I remained in the Bay Area after my career was over because this part of the world holds so many special memories for me and my family. When you experience so many life-changing or life-shaping moments in one place, it is almost impossible to pack up and leave.

I am still part of the Bay Area community, and I consider myself still part of the 49ers' family. My eight seasons with the 49ers were incredible. It really was a great ride, and you can be sure that I will always be a 49er.

My Final Game

After winning a second straight Super Bowl, everybody around San Francisco and the NFL was talking about a "three-peat."

We made it to the NFC championship game after the 1990 season and looked as if we might be heading back to the Super Bowl. Unfortunately, we didn't get that chance.

The New York Giants were hanging tough against us, trailing 13-12 late in the game. We were moving the ball well against their vaunted defense and getting into position to put the game away.

But the worst thing that could ever happen to a running back happened to me. Just as I received a handoff from Steve Young, I was met in the backfield by defensive tackle Erik Howard, who had gotten through unblocked.

Howard's helmet struck the ball just as it was being tucked into my arms. The ball popped loose and Lawrence Taylor recovered it at the Giants' 43-yard line with 2:36 remaining. Giants quarterback Jeff Hostetler completed a couple of passes, and then Matt Bahr kicked a 42-yard field goal as time expired to beat us 15-13.

Words of Encouragement

Obviously, it was the most difficult game of my career. I was heartbroken.

Ronnie Lott embraced me in the locker room, and I'll forever love him for how he treated me. He hugged me and said, "Everything is going to be all right." I cried like a baby.

That is everything you need to know about Ronnie Lott as a person. Nobody in that locker room was a bigger competitor than Ronnie, yet he went out of his way to show me our friendship meant more to him than a football game.

Ronnie's words gave me the strength to walk out of that damn place that day. I was shattered, but I also realized it just wasn't our day. We had the opportunity to win the thing and it just wasn't meant to be.

The one thing I've learned in life is you can't dwell on negative things. That is what I've always tried to focus on as an athlete. Walter Payton always told me to stay positive. He lived his life that way—even as he was dying from cancer a few years later. I have maintained a positive attitude throughout my life, as I'm a big proponent of motivational tapes. Listening to Tony Robbins and Dr. Emmett Miller of Stanford helped me relax and focus on the job at hand.

The fumble and its aftermath helped me refocus on things that are important in life. I treated it as a hurdle in life. It was something that happened, and I had to deal with it and not let it keep me down.

Whenever something negative happened, I always tried to counteract that with something positive. That is how I rehabilitated myself. I wasn't about to let that one bad play crush my career.

It's not a nasty word—"fumble"—it's just part of the game.

I had family and friends to help me get through that situation. And I knew I couldn't second-guess myself for anything I did leading up to that play. I was mentally tough and I trained as hard as I possibly could in the off season. I had been on three Super Bowl-winning teams, so I'd been to the mountaintop and I knew what it took to get there.

I can honestly say I was never out of shape in my life. I could not look back and say, "I wish I had done this" or "I wish I had done that." I wouldn't have changed a thing in my career.

Shocking News

The day after the disheartening loss to the Giants, I was already beginning to think about ways I could redeem myself the following season. Any time in my career when I had a bad play, I had always come back with even more determination.

But this time I would not get a chance to avenge myself. I was already stunned by what happened the day before when someone came down to the locker room and told Ronnie Lott and me that Coach George Seifert wanted to see us.

It had to be an uncomfortable situation for George, but he told us we had to be placed on Plan B. In other words, the team had let us go.

It was obvious to me owner Eddie DeBartolo made the decision on emotion. And all this time I thought Eddie was a friend of mine. I had a fumble and Ronnie did not have a great game, so Eddie decided to get rid of both of us.

Coach George Seifert (center) told me I would be placed on Plan B, but I know owner Eddie DeBartolo (left) was the one who made the decision. Carmen Policy is also pictured here, at the announcement the team was parting ways with George. (Photo by Brad Mangin)

The weirdest thing was they could not wait a week to let things calm down a little. They told us the next day that we did not fit into the team's plan. The next freakin' day!

I was absolutely stunned. I got into my car and I couldn't feel anything. I was in a fog on my drive home. I don't even know if the car was moving. Everything was in slow motion.

Opening Can of Worms

Things changed within the 49ers' organization after Ronnie and I were cut loose. The days of Camelot were over.

Looking back on it, I made a mistake when I kept such a close friendship with the owner of the team. Football is a business, and he took advantage of our friendship. In 1988, he said he was going to take care of me with a new contract. I was one of the elite runners in the league, and I got a new deal.

While it was a good contract, it wasn't nearly as good as what it could have been. But Eddie DeBartolo was my friend. I wasn't going to battle him over a few dollars because I trusted he would give me a fair shake.

Up until that time, very few 49ers players held out for new contracts because they trusted the organization. After that, things began to change. Ronnie and I were two respected leaders on the team. When they treated us like that, the players could see that there was no loyalty in the organization.

They opened up a can of worms. That is why they brought Dwight Clark in as general manager in the mid-'90s, as the team tried to cater once again to the players and regain their trust.

But the fact of the matter is that Eddie went off and made an emotional decision in the heat of the moment. That decision hurt the franchise and it hurt the fans of the 49ers.

I know Coach Walsh would never have gotten rid of us like that. In fact, Walsh expressed dismay over the decision made by his old team. He told one national publication: "You hope there wasn't a miscalculation made somewhere by somebody. I'm not privy to it, but I'm sure they have a plan."

Another PR Disaster

I don't know what the 49ers were thinking, but in February after Ronnie and I had been let go, the team decided to change the logo on its helmet. The 49ers were an organization of great tradition, and that tradition was going out the window.

Eddie DeBartolo and Carmen Policy sat in front of a bank of reporters and cameras to unveil the team's new look. It was so bizarre. The helmet looked cartoonish. Instead of the stylish, intertwined "SF," the helmet would now feature an oversized "49" with small block letters "ERS."

Coming so soon after our disappointing loss to the Giants, and the team parting ways with two of its most recognizable players, this latest development bombed in the Bay Area. The media and fans caused an uproar over the change in design. And just like Coca-Cola went back to "Coke Classic" after its ill-fated attempt at a new recipe, the 49ers were shamed into scrapping the new logo and returning to the old helmet.

Rapport with Eddie

Eddie DeBartolo was a good owner. He generally took care of the players, and everything was first class. Eddie demanded a lot from his employees. Everybody was expected to perform, from the players to the coaches to the guys in the equipment room.

When Eddie's father, Edward Sr., bought the team, he made a point to stay out of Bill Walsh's way. Eddie took his father's advice and stayed out of the picture, too. He generally let Walsh run the show. But Eddie really screwed up in the way he handled the departures of Ronnie, me, Joe Montana, Bill Walsh, George Seifert, Charles Haley, Michael Carter, and others.

He did things on emotion, rather than thinking them out rationally.

It was sort of funny to see Ronnie and Eddie on the same stage during the 2003 season when the 49ers retired Ronnie's No. 42 jersey. Eddie made his first appearance at Candlestick Park since his legal problems forced him to hand control of the team over to his sister, Denise DeBartolo York, and her husband, Dr. John York.

Ronnie and Eddie embraced. They butted heads quite a bit when Ronnie was a player. But now they've developed a good relationship. When I see Eddie, I still treat him with respect. But it's just not the same as it was throughout the 1980s.

Ronnie Lott puts his arm around former owner Eddie DeBartolo during a ceremony in 2003 to retire Ronnie's number. Current owner Dr. John York (behind the jersey) is in control of the team now. (Photo by Brad Mangin)

The Other Side

I played 11 seasons in the NFL, and I made the playoffs every season. It didn't really come as a surprise to me that the 49ers failed to earn a playoff spot in 1991 without Ronnie Lott and me.

We both signed with the Los Angeles Raiders for the 1991 season. Meanwhile, the 49ers were in total disarray. We played against the 49ers in the fifth week of the regular season. It was strange to play against my old team. I felt sick to my stomach because I was battling against my brothers.

We—the Raiders, that is—won that game 12-6 at the L.A. Coliseum, but it was not gratifying to beat the 49ers. It was just weird. Ronnie was lighting people up, and I ran hard and played well. Still, it was hard to get too excited about winning that game.

Across the way, in the 49ers' locker room, it was obvious they still considered us part of their team. After the game, Charles Haley was throwing a tantrum in the 49ers' locker room, mostly directed at quarterback Steve Young.

People with the 49ers knew the only person Charles respected enough to get through to him was Ronnie. So Ronnie had to leave the Raiders' locker room to get Charles to calm down before he hurt somebody or himself.

Returning to the Fold

After finishing my career with two seasons in Minnesota, I wanted to do something for the fans who had given me overwhelming support during my eight seasons with the 49ers.

I became the first player in the history of the league to return to his original team for the sole purpose of retiring. I got a letter from NFL commissioner Paul Tagliabue, saying it was the most refreshing thing he had seen in quite a while.

I had called Eddie DeBartolo and Carmen Policy to let them know what I wanted to do. It seemed to me that when a lot of guys who had played a long time for one team ended up retiring with another team, they sort of faded away. I wanted the opportunity rejoin the 49ers for just one day so people would always remember me as a member of the 49ers.

I think I had a special rapport with the fans of San Francisco, and I always wanted to be associated with the organization. It was definitely the right thing to do.

The gesture started a trend. At least three other players soon followed my lead. Eugene Lockhart returned to the Cowboys after finishing with the Houston Oilers; Art Monk came back to the Redskins after playing with the Philadelphia Eagles; and Leonard Marshall retired as a New York Giant after wrapping up his career with the Jets.

In the 1994 season, I had a definite rooting interest in the 49ers, even though I was no longer playing in the NFL. I was locked into the organization, and my signed contract meant I was enrolled in the team's benefits package for the season. I went to the games and sat in a luxury suite, and I thoroughly enjoyed watching the 49ers win their first Super Bowl since my playing days.

Comeback Kid?

Although I was completely satisfied with my life as a retired football player, late in the 1995 season it looked for a time as if I might be coming back to help my old team.

The 49ers had suffered a rash of injuries to their running backs, and they were forced to start Adam Walker at fullback in spite of a broken thumb.

Everybody with the 49ers knew I was still working out and in great shape. Eddie DeBartolo called to ask if I would be willing to come out of retirement for the end of the season and the playoffs. I talked it over with my wife, and we agreed that if the 49ers wanted me to play, I would play.

Coach Walsh, who was helping offensive coordinator Marc Trestman with the offense, invited me to his office in Menlo Park. He put me through a workout with some quarterbacks with whom he was working, including former Heisman Trophy winner Gino Torretta.

After looking at me run and catch passes, Coach Walsh told me, "Roger, you can still do it."

Then general manager Dwight Clark came out and timed me in the 40. I ran a 4.5 the first time he timed me and a 4.6 the second time. I had not absorbed a hit since the 1993 season, and I felt I could be explosive again on the football field.

The 49ers put me on retainer. They paid me for three weeks to continue to work out and be ready for when they would need me. They wanted me for about 15 plays a game to run some draws and catch some passes out of the backfield.

The phone call never came. Coach George Seifert did not want to sign me because he was so superstitious he did not want to make such a dramatic and bold change on the team so late in the year. It's too bad, because I felt I was ready to play some football.

Maybe they could have used me. The 49ers opened the playoffs at home against the Green Bay Packers. On the first play of the game, Steve Young threw a swing pass to Walker, who caught the ball and fumbled because of his broken thumb. The fumble was returned 31 yards for a touchdown, giving the Packers the momentum in a game they would win 27-17.

Just Give Me a Chance

After I trained so hard at the end of the season, I began think-ing maybe I could help out the team. I got the itch to compete again at the age of 35. My agent, Jim Steiner, talked to the 49ers about returning to Rocklin for another summer of training camp.

I did not expect the 49ers to give me anything. All I want-ed was a chance to compete for a job. If I was the best man and could help my team, fine. If the 49ers had someone better, that was fine, too.

I was in such great shape, it would have been nice to get an opportunity to return to the team. But I was also at peace with never playing football again. I knew it was a long shot that they would offer to take me to training camp.

When it didn't happen, I wasn't disappointed, because I really didn't get my hopes up.

Marathon Man

I consider myself lucky I left the game in such great physical condition. After all, with as much pounding as my body took during my 11-year career, I could easily have been in bad shape like some of my former teammates. Since my career has con-cluded, I haven't slowed down much. I still run like a maniac. I weigh 205 pounds and I've taken up running marathons. I put in about 45 miles of running a week to get ready for my foray into marathons. It's one of those things in life I feel I have to accomplish. Some people want to parachute out of planes, some people want to ski down the face of a steep mountain, some people want to go deep-sea diving. Me? I want to run some marathons. My goal is to run at least five marathons in my life.

I could've started running marathons sooner, but I'm making it a priority now. I have the time to train, and I'm ready for this new challenge in my life.

Hall of Fame?

I have been eligible for induction into the Pro Football Hall of Fame since 1999, and I have been a nominee every year since.

People always ask me if I get frustrated every year when my name isn't announced for inclusion into the select group. Believe it or not, the answer is no.

My patience is another of my best attributes. I would love to someday be standing on the stage in Canton, Ohio, being canonized as one of the all-time great players to ever step on a football field. But I am not going to waste a lot of time worrying about it, because I have a lot of other stuff going on in my life.

After all, I have won three Super Bowl championships, so that in itself is something that very few players have ever accomplished. If I get into the Hall of Fame soon, that would be great. If I get in later, that would be great, too.

There have been a lot of fantastic players who had to wait a long time to make it into the Hall of Fame. Heck, former Pittsburgh Steelers receiver Lynn Swann was not voted into the Hall until his 14th turn. Paul Hornung made it on his 12th try, and guard Tom Mack was not selected until his 11th.

Former 49ers linebacker Dave Wilcox's final season in the NFL was 1974, yet he was not selected until 2000—the same year Joe Montana and Ronnie Lott were also inducted into the Hall of Fame.

My biggest contribution to the game was opening people's eyes to the importance of using a running back to catch passes.

Just like waiting for a hole to develop, I realize I'm going to have to exercise some patience when it comes to being inducted into the Pro Football Hall of Fame. (Photo by Brad Mangin)

I still rank in the top 25 all-time in yards from scrimmage—a combination of rushing and receiving yards.

But at the time I retired, I was ninth in NFL history in that statistic. Eight of those players—Walter Payton, Tony Dorsett, Eric Dickerson, Jim Brown, Franco Harris, John Riggins and O.J. Simpson—are already in the Hall of Fame.

When I retired, I led all of those Hall of Fame running backs in receptions and receiving yards. It was a huge honor when I overtook my idol, Walter Payton, for the lead among all running backs. Payton amassed 492 receptions for 4,538 yards in his career.

I finished with 566 catches for 4,911 yards—with 508 of those catches coming with the 49ers. I rank behind only Jerry Rice and Terrell Owens in receptions in 49ers history.

When I had my 1,000 rushing-1,000 receiving season, I was a fullback and made the Pro Bowl. I also blocked for a 1,000-yard rusher, Wendell Tyler, as a fullback and later became a 1,000-yard rusher at fullback and halfback. There aren't many players who have made the Pro Bowl at fullback and halfback.

I worked hard and never missed a practice. I had control over my own performance for my career. But when it comes to the Hall of Fame, obviously I have no control over it. Some of the voters have expressed that a new procedure must be put into place to more fairly determine which players make it and which players do not.

I'll just continue to be patient and let them judge for themselves how my performance and my skills impacted the sport. It would be a great way to top off my career. But I'll always have those three Super Bowl rings in my safe-deposit box as validation of my football career.

Chapter 6

BEFORE AND AFTER ROGER

To a lot of people who consider themselves fans of the San Francisco 49ers, the team's history begins in 1981. But one thing I learned from my involvement with the organization is there were a lot of great teams and great players wearing 49ers colors before the team started winning Super Bowls.

When Joe Thomas was hired as the general manager in 1977, he wanted to make a complete break from the past. For some insane reason, he ordered the removal of anything historical from the 49ers' team offices in Redwood City.

Can you imagine? The organization wanted to sever ties with all the great 49ers of the past, including Hall of Famers Leo Nomellini, Joe Perry, Hugh McElhenny, Y.A. Tittle, John Henry Johnson, Bob St. Clair, Jimmy Johnson and Dave Wilcox.

All those players—and many more outstanding players of their eras—were part of the 49ers before there were any Super Bowl trophies displayed in the lobby of the team offices.

The 49ers have a rich tradition. In today's NFL with the salary cap and such an importance placed on players changing teams on a yearly basis, it will be impossible for any franchise to do what the 49ers of the 1980s were able to accomplish.

Fans of the 49ers will have to learn to live with a team that might not make the playoffs every season, as the team did when I played in San Francisco.

The 49ers have some smart people in charge. I think Dr. John York is going to turn the organization into a successful operation that succeeds off the field as well as on the field. But it is not always going to be easy.

The club parted ways with some notable veterans in 2004. Players such as Jeff Garcia, Terrell Owens, Garrison Hearst and Derrick Deese have seen their days with the 49ers come to an end. Now the 49ers have to move on and find a way to get the job done with a bunch of fresh faces.

Even during the days of Eddie DeBartolo, the game of football was not won by the team that spent the most money. The building block for success is the draft. A team has to draft the right players, then develop them properly. It is up to the coaching staff to place those individuals into the roles that best utilize their skills. Then it's up to the front office to hold on to those players for the long haul. That is how a team builds continuity and wins football games.

The draft has always been the key. Just think about it: Joe Montana was selected in the third round, Dwight Clark was taken in the 10th round, John Taylor, Charles Haley and Steve Wallace were picked after the opening of the third round, and I was chosen late in the second round.

There are always a lot of impact players to be found after the first round of the draft; you just have to know where to look. That was what Bill Walsh's 49ers did better than any team in the league.

The ability to draft quality players will ultimately determine if the 49ers can add to those five Super Bowl trophies in the future.

Embracing the Alumni

Of Coach Bill Walsh's many contributions to the 49ers, one that is easy to overlook came upon his hiring in 1979. Walsh created a new administrative position and filled the opening with popular former 49ers receiver R.C. Owens. His job was to bring back the alumni, which had been shunned by the previous regime. Owens would serve as coordinator until 2001 after 22 years on the job. He died in 2012, at age 77, but left a lasting legacy.

"Bill hired me because the relationships between the organization and the former players had been lost," R.C. once said: "A team's alumni is so important to an organization. Those players, beginning in '46 and through the '50s, '60s and '70s are the foundation of the 49ers."

The 49ers became the first NFL team to organize an annual alumni day when ex-players are invited back to a game and introduced to the crowd at halftime.

Alley-Oop Is Born

You can't turn on a basketball game without hearing the announcers talk about an "alley-oop pass." R.C. Owens should be getting royalties, because he is responsible for bringing it into the sports lexicon.

While practicing to face the Los Angeles Rams in the second week of the 1957 season, the six-foot-three Owens realized he could jump and reach higher than most defensive backs. Offensive coordinator Red Hickey quickly inserted the deep pass into the playbook. All quarterback Y.A. Tittle had to do was throw the ball high in the air, and Owens would go get it.

"San Francisco fans stood twice during the course of a game: once for the National Anthem and once for the alley-oop pass," Owens once said.

The first playoff touchdown in 49ers history came, appropriately enough, in 1957 when Owens outjumped Detroit cornerback James David to catch a 34-yard pass from Tittle.

A dictionary, *America's Listening*, lists one of its definitions of "alley oop" as a long, high-arcing pass. "It was originally made famous by R.C. Owens catching such passes from Tittle," the entry reads. It was also the name of a comic strip that dates to 1933.

Owens's extraordinary leaping ability also resulted in one of the rarest sights in NFL history. In 1962, while with the Baltimore Colts, Owens was standing under the goal posts (then located on the goal line) when Washington's Bob Khayat lined up for a 40-yard field goal attempt. As the line-drive kick was about to split the uprights, Owens jumped high in the air and swatted the ball away to block the attempt. Two years later, the NFL outlawed the strategy. Now, a kick can be blocked only at the line of scrimmage.

Raw Meat Lover

One of the great characters of the past was tackle Bob St. Clair, who played for the 49ers from 1953 to '63. He was a giant playing the game during a time when players were much smaller than they are today.

At six foot eight, St. Clair blocked 10 field goal attempts during the 1956 season. He once lost five teeth while blocking a punt. Losing those teeth must have been scary, considering how this man loves to eat.

Aside from his prodigious football talent, St. Clair is also well known for his eating habits. St. Clair eats meat only one way: raw. Last year during a luncheon honoring some former 49ers, he ordered a New York strip. He asked that it be brought out uncooked.

"They asked, 'Do you want us to char it just a little?'" St. Clair said. "I said, 'Of course not. I want it right out of the ice box onto the plate.'"

St. Clair's preference for raw meat virtually guaranteed he had an entire table to himself during most training camp meals.

"I was his roommate and I refused to eat with him," Y.A. Tittle said. "How would you like to sit with someone who's eating raw liver?"

St. Clair's Field

Before the 49ers moved into Candlestick Park in 1971, they called Kezar Stadium home.

St. Clair played more games (189) at Kezar Stadium than any other football player. He lined up at offensive tackle on the seagull-infested grounds while with Polytechnic High School, University of San Francisco and, of course, with the 49ers.

Today, the field, located in Golden Gate Park, is still used for high school football games. It bears the name "Bob St. Clair Field."

Obviously, St. Clair has more memories of that place than anyone else. One of his favorite memories at old Kezar came in 1964 when Minnesota's Jim Marshall picked up a fumble and ran the wrong way for a safety. The 49ers still lost that game 27-22.

Another of his most vivid memories includes quite a blooper that he committed himself.

In the late 1950s, in one of the 49ers' non-playoff seasons, the fans were particularly fickle. Quarterback Y.A. Tittle regularly fielded the brunt of abuse from the hometown fans.

Tired of hearing all the boos directed his way, Tittle asked St. Clair to break from tradition and be the first player to run onto the field out of the east tunnel.

"I did him a favor because he didn't want to get booed," St. Clair said.

When St. Clair jogged out of the tunnel, he was bombarded with a cascade of boos, he said. Already a little flustered from the uproar from the unhappy fans, St. Clair stubbed his cleats on the wood lip that bordered the playing field.

St. Clair—all six foot eight, 245 pounds of him—went tumbling to the turf. That's right, he took a nose dive on the same lush grass that would one day be named after him.

"Everybody in the stands was laughing so hard that when Y.A. came out, they weren't booing," St. Clair said.

Now that's the definition of a team player.

Tittle Town

Y.A. Tittle was a Hall of Fame quarterback and a tough competitor. There's that famous picture of him on the ground with blood all over his face. That photo epitomizes the ferocity with which he played the game. He was a true warrior.

Today, he runs a successful insurance company in the Bay Area, and his competitiveness has carried over into the business world. He runs his company like a football team to get the most out of his sales team.

He is still a quarterback; it's just not on the football field any more.

"The Jet" Takes Off

I enjoyed watching film of some of the pioneers, as I liked to call them. Joe "The Jet" Perry was a member of the famed Million Dollar Backfield, along with halfbacks Hugh McElhenny and John Henry Johnson and quarterback Y.A. Tittle. Every member of that backfield is in the Pro Football Hall of Fame.

Perry died in 2011 at age 84. For many years, he always played in my golf tournament in Iowa, and he kept telling me I was going to break his team record for rushing yards. If I had a few more games, I might have gotten him, but he still holds that mark with 7,344 yards. I'm in second on the all-time 49ers list with 7,064 yards.

He was an explosive runner—just plain fast. His nickname was very appropriate because he would hit that hole like he was being propelled by a jet engine. Watching film of him, he made everybody else look like they were in slow motion.

Long-Awaited Meeting

I always wanted to meet Hugh McElhenny, but I never got the chance during my playing days. Finally, I met him on a beach in Hawaii in 2000.

I went to Hawaii for the Pro Bowl, and I happened to be walking next to the ocean when I heard somebody say, "There's Hugh McElhenny." I couldn't believe it, because I'd watched a lot of film of him.

He was the best broken-field runner to ever play the game, in my opinion. He used to make people look stupid, and I'd be sitting there watching it thinking, "How did he make that move?" He ran in such an instinctive way in the open field it was almost as if he had eyes in the back of his head.

When I heard Hugh McElhenny's name, I was like a little kid. I was all excited because this was my first chance to meet a hero.

I went up to him and introduced myself and told him, "I've been wanting to meet you for so long." He told me he had been wanting to meet me, too. It was so cool. It made my day to meet that man.

He was a beautiful runner. We had a lot in common, too. He ran the hurdles in high school and won the California championship. That background carried him far on the football field.

Leo the Lion

I loved to talk to the pioneers about what it was like to play back in the 1950s and '60s. Back in those days, players did not make enough money during the season to sustain them year-round.

In the off season, Hall of Fame offensive and defensive tackle Leo Nomellini earned money as a professional wrestler. It helped him remain in good shape during the off season, too. He played in every 49ers game for 14 years, a streak that reached 174 consecutive games. He wanted everybody to know he was one tough son of a bitch. He was mean. Nobody wanted to mess with him, and that gave him a great advantage on the football field.

Leo considered quitting football to concentrate on wrestling year-round, because he made $22,000 annually playing football and $28,000 as a wrestler. Nomellini's big wrestling rival was world champion Lou Thesz. In five matches, Leo had one draw, three defeats and one short-lived victory.

In 1955, the two men squared off in front of 12,000 fans at the Cow Palace. Thesz threw "The Lion" from the ring and then kicked him repeatedly, not allowing him to get back between the ropes. Thesz was disqualified, and Leo was crowned champion. But two days later, the National Wrestling Alliance, apparently in an attempt to gain more publicity, announced a champion could not lose his crown due to a disqualification.

"The rest of us knew it was staged, but we didn't tell Leo," former 49ers end Billy Wilson told the *Oakland Tribune.* "He threatened a couple of guys, asking them, 'You want to get in the ring with me?'"

Leo died in October 2000 from complications involving a stroke. He was 76.

Old No. 33

Of course, I have an affinity for anyone who wears No. 33. One of my favorite old-time 49ers is Hardy Brown, who played middle linebacker from 1951 to '56 and wore the uniform number I would be issued three decades later.

Hardy was known for his brutal style of tackling the ball carrier. Instead of wrapping them up, he would just level them with his unorthodox shoulder tackle. Because this was before the time of facemasks, many times, Hardy would knock players out of the game.

As you could imagine, Hardy was not exactly popular among the other teams. The Philadelphia Eagles put a bounty on Hardy. They collected $500, which would go to the player who knocked him out of the game. Instead, it was Hardy who should have collected the bounty. He escaped the game unscathed and knocked out three of their players while they were trying to get him.

Owner Collapses

When Joe Perry is asked about his most enduring memory of Kezar Stadium, nearly five decades later he still gets a little emotional. During a game in 1957, Perry said he looked up into the stands and saw 49ers founder and co-owner Tony Morabito suffer a fatal heart attack.

"We got word that Tony had died," Perry said. "The mood turned pretty somber. You could hear people crying. We all loved him."

Perry regained his composure after learning at halftime the 49ers owner had passed away. The 49ers rallied to pull off a 21-17 victory over the Chicago Bears that day. Four years earlier, Perry rushed for 1,018 yards, which inspired Morabito to give him a $5 bonus for every yard. In 1953, a bonus of $5,090 went a long way.

Wilcox Honored

In 2000, linebacker Dave Wilcox was selected to the Pro Football Hall of Fame more than a quarter-century after playing his final game with the 49ers. His induction might have been overshadowed a bit by Joe Montana and Ronnie Lott, both of whom entered the Hall that same year.

Wilcox was nicknamed "The Intimidator" for his hard-nosed style of play. He was a ferocious hitter.

"In the NFL, there are usually around five or six players during a season that nobody wants to mess with," said former 49ers middle linebacker Frank Nunley. "Deacon Jones was one; Dick Butkus was another; and Dave Wilcox was another guy that nobody ever wanted to get mad."

Quarterback John Brodie said having Wilcox on the field eliminated the tight end from opposing offenses. Safety Mel Phillips said Wilcox preserved his career because nobody ever made it past Wilcox to block him. And when asked about Wilcox's deservedness for the Hall of Fame, Butkus asked, "Who was better?"

But, interestingly, many 49ers fans were just hearing about him when he shared the spotlight with Joe and Ronnie in Canton, Ohio.

He realized when he played for the 49ers, the organization was not as popular as when he received the ultimate honor.

"I played before Joe and money," Wilcox said during his induction speech.

Len Eshmont

Beginning in 1957, the 49ers annually honor the team's most inspirational and courageous player. What makes the award special is everybody in the locker room has a vote.

The Len Eshmont Award began just a few months after Eshmont died in May of 1957 from infectious hepatitis at the age of 39. Eshmont played on the original 49ers team in 1946 and retired just three years later. He was the head coach at the University of Virginia when he died.

Eshmont was a football legend on the East Coast, where he enrolled at Fordham. Eshmont enabled Fordham to continue as a football powerhouse after he joined the team in 1936. After an All-America senior year, he signed to play with the New York Giants. He played one season with the Giants before he was commissioned in the U.S. Navy, where he served as a physical education instructor at the naval preflight schools around the country, including at St. Mary's in Moraga.

Eshmont starred on the Navy football teams. After leaving the Navy, he decided to remain in the Bay Area to join the 49ers, a new team forming in the All-America Football Conference.

He retired after the 1949 season, just as the 49ers were preparing to join the NFL, to begin his coaching career.

Running Watters

Of course, I paid particularly close attention to the running backs that followed me with the 49ers. I liked Ricky Watters a lot.

He really developed into a tough runner. A lot of times early in his career, he did too much shaking and baking and tried too many fancy cuts. But as he got older and stronger and bigger, he started attacking defenses better.

Ricky's problem was his impatience. In this offense, you had to be patient and eventually your time would come. He wanted to run the ball. But in the 49ers' system, a running back didn't run the ball that much. The focus was on being a complete player.

His finest game with the 49ers was probably his last game. In Super Bowl XXIX, Ricky tied my record with three touchdowns in a 49-26 victory over the San Diego Chargers. He caught a 51-yard scoring pass, had an eight-yard TD, and added a nine-yard run.

Unfortunately, Ricky did not endear himself to his offensive linemen. He had some bad things to say about them, and they did not care for him. But Ricky had the ability to do everything pretty well. After helping the 49ers to the Super Bowl and leading the team in rushing for three straight seasons, he bolted for the big money the Philadelphia Eagles threw his way.

Change in Philosophy

When Steve Mariucci took over in 1997, the 49ers became more of a running team. Technically, it was still the West Coast Offense the team was using, but Mariucci had spent time on the L.A. Rams' coaching staff under John Robinson, and it showed.

Garrison Hearst developed into a pure runner in Mariucci's system. Garrison is a tough, hard-nosed runner who makes things happen. I admire Garrison because of the way he fought back after two very serious injuries.

As a rookie with the Arizona Cardinals in 1993, he played just six games before going down with a season-ending injury. The next year, he played just eight games and rushed for less than 200 yards because of another knee injury.

But Garrison bounced back in 1995, rushing for 1,070 yards and earning league-wide recognition as Comeback Player of the Year.

The 49ers' offensive system changed gradually under the different head coaches, from Bill Walsh (left) to George Seifert (right) to Steve Mariucci (center). (Photo by Brad Mangin)

He looked as if he had turned his career around with two more 1,000-yard seasons with the 49ers. In 1998, Garrison broke my 49ers single-season rushing record with 1,570 yards. I gained 1,502 yards in 1988.

In a playoff game in Atlanta, Garrison suffered a broken left ankle. Because of complications from the fracture, he had to miss two full seasons and looked as if he might never play again.

But Garrison would again earn the Comeback Player of the Year honor after rushing for 1,206 yards in 2001.

B.Y., the Leader

When outstanding young linebacker Julian Peterson won the Len Eshmont Award for the 2003 season, he was surprised. "I just thought that was the Bryant Young Award," he said.

It seems that way, doesn't it? I consider myself fortunate enough to have won the Eshmont twice during my career. Bryant Young won it four times, including in 1999 when it looked as if his career might be over.

In a game late in the 1998 season against the Giants, Bryant sustained a grisly broken leg when teammate Ken Norton Jr.'s helmet struck his lower leg, which was firmly planted in the ground. The force of the blow broke Bryant's right tibia and fibula.

He underwent three operations in 17 days and never left the hospital. Bryant had complications from the first surgery, had a titanium rod inserted in his leg, and landed in intensive care with a 103 temperature.

Bryant worked hard to get back into shape. He came back to start all 16 games the following season, recording 11 sacks. He followed that up with 9.5 sacks in 2000. He was a leader and inspiration for that organization before retiring after the 2007 season. He was always a soft-spoken guy, but when he had something to say to the team, he spoke volumes.

Gritty Garcia

Quarterback Jeff Garcia had a fantastic five-year run with the 49ers, but the club felt it was in its best interest to move on without him in 2004.

I liked Jeff a lot, and I don't doubt that he could have helped the team in 2004, but sometimes tough decisions have to be made. Things turned out okay for him. He went on to be a steady and reliable NFL quarterback for the Cleveland Browns, Detroit Lions, Philadelphia Eagles (twice) and Tampa Bay Buccaneers. Jeff even made one more Pro Bowl at age 37, when he had a strong year for the 2007 Buccaneers.

What I remember most about Jeff is the way he overcame a great deal of adversity to earn trips to the Pro Bowl in three straight years. When he came to the 49ers in 1999, he was basically thrown to the wolves after Steve Young experienced his career-ending concussion.

Jeff was not ready to take over as the quarterback, but the team had no other choice. He ran for his life for most of the season before he slowly started to figure out the complexities of the system.

I remember seeing him early the next season after a loss to the Carolina Panthers, a game in which he got benched in favor of Rick Mirer. He was down in the dumps. I told him to keep his head up and keep fighting. I knew he was a leader and could snap out of it. "Everything will come together," I told him. "Believe in your ability."

The next week, he started an incredible string of successes in a game against the St. Louis Rams. Jeff finished the season

Jeff Garcia overcame a lot of obstacles to put together three Pro Bowl seasons, keeping alive the quarterback tradition of Joe Montana and Steve Young. (Photo by Brad Mangin)

with 31 touchdown passes and just 10 interceptions and was named to his first NFC Pro Bowl team.

Jeff is a good kid. I'm amazed at how far he came and what he has endured in his life, losing two siblings at early ages. He's been through a lot in his life, so a little adversity on the football field is easy for him to overcome.

Big Shoes to Fill

Jeff Garcia knew what he was getting into, but he tried to live the dream.

He grew up in Gilroy, just south of San Jose, and grew up a fan of the 49ers. As a quarterback, he paid close attention to Joe Montana and Steve Young.

One time while he was still playing at San Jose State, Jeff happened to bump into Jerry Rice in a nightspot. Jeff, who never lacked for confidence, strode up to the established NFL superstar and declared, "Someday I'll be throwing passes to you with the 49ers."

Sure enough, Jeff got his wish when he was forced into the starting lineup just three games into the 1999 season. Jeff threw seven touchdown passes to Jerry, before the greatest receiver in NFL history moved to the Oakland Raiders for the 2001 season.

But Jeff also experienced the harsh realities of following the succession of great 49ers quarterbacks. It is difficult to live up to the play of Joe and Steve, but Jeff did a pretty good job of it with three consecutive trips to the Pro Bowl.

Still, he admitted the burden often was a little too much. In the off season after his final game with the 49ers, Jeff said there were definite advantages and disadvantages to playing professionally so close to home.

"I have always looked at my position with the 49ers as really wanting to be that next guy in the lineage of quarterbacks," Jeff said. "I always tried to prove myself in a positive way. ... It's almost like you can never do enough to please. At some point, that starts to get old."

Jeff believes he was never fully accepted by 49ers fans, who have come to expect greatness out of their quarterbacks. Steve Young was never fully embraced until he won his first Super Bowl.

The 49ers were lucky to get Jeff. After all, he came to the team as the 49ers hit their lowest point since the pre-Bill Walsh days with a 4-12 record in 1999. Jeff also supplied one of the great 49ers comebacks of all time, when he rallied the club from a 24-point deficit late in the fourth quarter to pull off a remarkable 39-38 playoff victory over the New York Giants.

Oh, man, it's always nice to hang a playoff loss on the New York Giants, isn't it? In that game, Jeff threw for 331 yards and three touchdowns and threw two two-point conversions. That's the stuff legends are made of, except in San Francisco. Because of the standard that was set a long time ago, if you're a quarterback with the 49ers it's either Super Bowl or bust.

Jeff found himself a victim of the salary cap. Teams have to ask themselves if they're capable of winning now. If they're not, then they start building for the future, and that means getting rid of some of the veteran players who are making big salaries.

I don't like to see that, but that's the way it is. The players wanted it this way. Gene Upshaw and the players' union agreed to it, so now the players have to live with it. A lot of players are never able to fulfill their contracts because once their salaries get too high, the teams have a built-in excuse to release them.

Quarterback Pressure

How difficult is it to succeed as a quarterback with the 49ers? Just ask Elvis Grbac.

Elvis was a very good backup to Steve Young in the mid-1990s. He was being groomed as possibly the quarterback of the future, and he proved he could be a very efficient player when Young was injured in the 1995 and '96 seasons.

In fact, Elvis led the 49ers to a 38-20 upset victory over the Dallas Cowboys in Texas Stadium in 1995 when it looked like the 49ers' playoff hopes were in jeopardy. But the next year, he did not get the glowing praise after he once again played against the Cowboys.

Elvis threw two costly interceptions against the Cowboys, who had knocked Steve Young out of the game with a concussion. San Francisco Mayor Willie Brown was in Paris but still weighed in with an opinion in a conference call with Bay Area reporters.

Mayor Brown said Elvis was "an embarrassment to humankind." Furthermore, Brown added Elvis "can't play in any stadium that I'm going to assist to be built."

Elvis, a Cleveland native, was standing in front of reporters the next day when Coach George Seifert shouted a question from behind the assemblage.

"Elvis," Seifert bellowed, "is it true the mayor of Cleveland called you and said he'd build a stadium for you there?"

Nearly a decade later, the Browns have a new money-making stadium—though Elvis never played there—and the 49ers are still trying to find a suitable permanent home.

Center Chris Dalman, who is one of Elvis's best friends, said players are accustomed to getting yelled at by fans. But this one was a little unique.

"It's amazing some of the things you hear fans yelling, hanging over the field, yelling," Dalman said. "But it's one thing for somebody angry at the game to yell something at Elvis and another for a politician across the world to do something like that. Maybe the president will take a shot at him next."

Elvis was the bigger man. He was going through some personal problems, his son having recently been diagnosed with spina bifida. A week or so later, the 49ers had their 50th Anniversary Gala, and Willie Brown apologized to him for his ill-timed remarks.

Still, Elvis could not have gotten out of San Francisco fast enough. That off season, Elvis became a free agent and signed a contract to become the starter for the Kansas City Chiefs.

Impressions of Owens

Terrell Owens spent his first eight seasons in San Francisco and put up some amazing statistics. He scored 83 touchdowns, more than anyone in 49ers history except Jerry Rice—who blew everyone away with 187.

I liked Terrell's attitude on the field. It was clear he played to win. But he certainly did not mind offending plenty of people off the field. And throughout his career, his immaturity continued to rub people the wrong way.

The important thing in football is getting respect from your teammates and treating other people with respect. The bottom line is that fame and money aren't important. What's important in life is being a good person. That's how people judge others. Terrell might not be remembered around the 49ers as being the most polite person to the media, but that isn't how it all began for the kid from the University of Tennessee-Chattanooga.

When he reported to training camp in the summer of 1996, he called all of his elders "Sir." He even addressed reporters in that way, until he was told that it wasn't necessary.

"I feel like it's respectful," Terrell said then. "I was always taught to say, 'Yes sir, no sir.' It's funny, in meetings here, a coach will ask a player a question and he'll answer, 'Yeah, yeah.' And it makes me want to tell them, 'You should say, sir.' They sound disrespectful. But I'm not in a position to tell them that yet."

Through the years, Terrell became a little more bold and outspoken. He ran to the star in the middle of Texas Stadium twice in the same game after scoring touchdowns against the Cowboys in 2000.

When Coach Steve Mariucci suspended him for a game without pay, Terrell felt the coach had betrayed him. The next year, after an overtime loss to the Chicago Bears, Owens blamed the defeat on the lack of a killer instinct—citing Mariucci's "buddy system" with some coaches around the league.

Former 49er receiver Terrell Owens, brought too much attention on himself with his outrageous statements and controversial actions during his time with the 49ers. (Photo by Brad Mangin)

Passing of the Torch

A lot of people did not realize Eddie DeBartolo and his sister each owned half of the team. That was the way Edward J. DeBartolo Sr. wanted it. And that's the way it was at the time of his death in 1994.

Eddie DeBartolo was the controlling owner of the team, while Denise DeBartolo York, his sister, was always content being out of the public eye.

Eddie's reign as owner of the 49ers began to unravel on him in December 1997 when he handed control of the organization to his sister, Denise DeBartolo York, after becoming the focus of a grand jury investigation into gaming fraud in Louisiana.

Fifteen months later, NFL commissioner Paul Tagliabue fined Eddie $1 million and suspended him indefinitely for conduct detrimental to the league. Because Eddie pleaded guilty to a felony—failure to report an extortion attempt—he was never reinstated as owner.

Denise and her husband, Dr. John York, acquired control of the 49ers from Eddie in exchange for stock and real estate holdings in April 2000, settling a bitter dispute between the parties. The DeBartolo Corp. purchased the 49ers in 1977 for $17 million, and Denise had been a silent part owner all along.

"People said that I stole the team from my brother and that John wanted it and made me do it," Denise said. "Any rational human being could see that I was in a situation I didn't create. I was in a position I never aspired to be in. I didn't want to see everything go down the tubes that my father had worked for."

Confidence in York

I've known Dr. John and Denise York for a long time—long before they ever had an inkling that they might take control of the 49ers from Eddie. I have a tremendous amount of respect for the York family. Their boys, Jed and Tony, always looked up to me. I remember giving Tony some pointers to get him ready for football season and advising him on different workouts.

After the Yorks took over the 49ers, they brought me in to do some things. One of my first assignments with the 49ers was to be a mentor to Lawrence Phillips, who was signed for the 1999 season when Garrison Hearst was lost for the season because of his ankle injury.

Lawrence went to Nebraska, and he wore No. 33 with the 49ers—just like me. I spent a lot of time with him during training camp to help him adjust to the 49ers. It worked for a little while, but then Lawrence went off in another direction. He had a bad argument with Coach Mariucci, who decided to release him in the middle of the season for "conduct detrimental to the team."

In recent years, I've worked with the 49ers from a marketing side, as I've used some of my connections in Silicon Valley. In essence, I was a business development guy with the organization.

During the season, I help host different companies and politicians in the owner's suite. Dr. York has done a great job of marketing the 49ers. He has recognized that NFL teams can't live entirely off the television contract, and he is reaching out to become a partner in the community.

Controversial Decision

Dr. John York gained a lot of notoriety around the nation when he fired Coach Mariucci after back-to-back playoff seasons. He said he wanted someone who would fit more into the structure of his organization.

Today, Dr. York said he does not regret the move to fire his coach. But he does admit to messing up the logistics of carrying out the decision.

It was the Monday after the 49ers' playoff loss to the Tampa Bay Buccaneers when Mariucci settled down with his family to watch an episode of the hit reality show *Joe Millionaire*. The phone rang and it was York on the line.

The two had a lengthy talk, and after it was concluded, Mariucci had the sense something was going to give.

Two days later, Dr. York summoned Mariucci to his office and relieved him of his coaching duties, citing philosophical differences. Mariucci had one year left on his contract. By the time Mariucci got out of his meeting with Dr. York, news had already spread he had been fired. Mariucci's wife, Gayle, had heard the reports on the radio and drove to the 49ers' facility in tears. She waited in her husband's office and was comforted by some players who had also caught wind of the major development.

"That was a mistake," Dr. York said. "It should not have happened that way. I have to take full responsibility for that. It was not as well planned as it should've been. There was clearly a miscommunication between me and other people who were working on that."

On the Same Page

In order to have a successful organization, everybody must be on the same page. You can't have the owner, general manager and head coach doing their own things. You have to be able to work things out and compromise. Coach Mariucci was on a different page than his owner and general manager Terry Donahue.

You never want to see any sort of fighting among team management. Those hard feelings sift down to the team. I think that's what took place with the 49ers and why a change was made. I don't think the firing of Coach Mariucci had anything to do with money. They should have been able to work out the details, because he did a good job as the coach.

But that's the way the business works. There are always issues that a lot of people never know about because they happen behind closed doors. It's like all forms of business. In the software business, it's the same way. If you don't put up the numbers and meet the quotas, you have to go in a different direction. Sometimes you have to bring in new people with new attitudes.

On the Run with Frank Gore

As he churned out yard after yard, running back Frank Gore passed me for second on the 49ers' all-time rushing list and then went on to surpass Joe "The Jet" Perry for the franchise record. And I was rooting for him the whole way. I love Frank Gore.

Here's a guy that has been a one-man show for so many years. During all those losing seasons before Jim Harbaugh arrived, Gore was the guy who kept the team together. He basically said, 'If you guys don't know how to win, I'm going to show you how to win." He was the anchor.

Frank has my respect because he's an all-around back. He takes pride in his blocking and does dozens of little things over the course of a game that the casual fan might not even notice.

There might be games when he has more than 150 rushing yards, but I'll go up to him and say: "I loved that block that you had." Or I'll pick out something else subtle and say, "You sold that play-action fake and fooled everybody." I know Frank takes pride in being a complete back.

I think Frank has learned a lot about his job from my old backfield mate, Tom Rathman, who became the 49ers running backs coach in 2009. Tom is an amazingly smart guy and was always sort of a coach on the field for us. He would overhear the offensive linemen making a call – and correct them because there were times he knew their assignments better than they did.

Tom took pride in his blocking. So if you want to play for the 49ers these days, you'd better block. Tom spends a lot of time teaching the art of picking up the blitz. And Frank just has a natural way of blocking. He's not that big – 5-foot-9 – but he just cold-cocks these linebackers and puts them on their backs.

The exciting thing for Frank is that he finally got a taste of the playoffs in 2011. After the 49ers clinched their spot in the postseason, I told him to be ready for a whole new wave of intensity. And after his first playoff game, Frank came up and said: "Roger, you were right. This game is fast now. The playoffs are a different speed."

Harbaugh Rights the Ship

Jim Harbaugh is definitely a special human being in my book. The highest compliment I can give him is this: He's a clone of Bill Walsh.

He reminds me of Bill in so many ways. He motivates players by holding them accountable for everything they do, on the field and off. Bill used to tell us that we were an extension of each other. Harbaugh emphasizes the same approach. He wants everyone in that locker room to have one heartbeat.

Jim also knows how to maximize the strength of every player on the roster, which was a big part of Bill's genius. In Harbaugh's case, there's no better example of that than what he did with Alex Smith.

Fans were ready to Alex run out of town. They'd seen enough disappointing play out of the 2005 No. 1 pick and they and wanted him gone. Instead Jim embraced him and said, "He's my guy." Those words alone – "He's my guy" — gave Alex some confidence. And that was all he needed, a little bit of confidence and support. Jim was the guy who did that. And Alex would run through a wall for him.

Harbaugh also recognized that one of Alex's strengths was rolling out and making throws on the move, so he gave him more freedom to do so. And as the season went on Alex gained more and more confidence.

Alex wasn't afraid anymore. His confidence grew every game. And he finished the season with only five interceptions, a 49ers record for the fewest in a season. That's amazing.

Whatever Jim was doing, it was working with Alex. It's sad that Bill Walsh is no longer here to see and enjoy Jim's success on so many levels.

Against the Odds

Jim Harbaugh showed the organization right off the bat that you'd better hop aboard his way of thinking. If you don't buy into the 49ers' way? Well, there's the door. Bill wouldn't tolerate any cancers on his team, and neither does Jim Harbaugh.

The 49ers signed Braylon Edwards, a veteran receiver, for 2011 but when he came in he wasn't exactly focused. He did some things that weren't to appropriate for the team. And because of that, Jim Harbaugh let him go.

And Braylon was a guy who had gone to Michigan, like Harbaugh, but that didn't buy him any extra slack. So that was an eye-opener right there. If that didn't wake up people, nothing would.

Harbaugh succeeded in his first season despite enormous hurdles. The 49ers gave him the job on January 7, 2011, but it looked like he was going to be handcuffed his first season. An NFL lockout wiped out the traditional minicamps and Organized Team Activities, so there was no chance for Harbaugh to implement his playbook until training camp opened on time in July.

Harbaugh adapted to the situation just as he did when he was an NFL quarterback – and he was no ordinary quarterback. He was a great player. Harbaugh played in the NFL from 1987-2000 and earned a spot on the Indianapolis Colts' Wall of Fame.

But the beauty of Jim Harbaugh is that coaching is in his DNA. His dad, Jack Harbaugh, was a longtime college coach and won a Division I-AA title at Western Kentucky. Jim and his brother John (now the Baltimore Ravens head coach) learned from an early age that coaching is all about relationships. How do you manage your assistants? How do you motivate players? I guarantee you that Jim learned those lessons at a very young age.

One of my favorite things about Harbaugh is that he made one of his dad's old sayings a rallying cry for the 49ers. Jim would ask his players, "Who's got it better than us?" And the players would answer, "Noooo-body!" That's the way Jim and John were taught to answer when Jack asked them that question as kids.

I love that slogan. In fact, I've got a banner with "Who's Got it Better Than Us?" hanging in my office.

The Birth of a New Dynasty?

What Harbaugh accomplished in his first season was truly amazing. He went 13-3, got the 49ers into the playoffs for the first time since 2002 and took them all the way to the NFC Championship game at Candlestick Park.

We didn't get to the Super Bowl. The New York Giants beat the 49ers in overtime before going on to topple the New England Patriots in Super Bowl XLVI. But up until that final chapter, Harbaugh's first season had so many parallels to the 1981 season that launched the 49ers dynasty.

With 1981, the play you think of is The Catch, with Dwight Clark snaring that 6-yard pass from Joe Montana with 51 seconds to beat the Dallas Cowboys in the NFC title game. In 2011, it was The Grab, with Vernon Davis catching a 14-yard pass from Alex with 9 seconds remaining against the New Orleans Saints in the divisional round.

In both seasons, there was a big shift in the defense. In '81, the 49ers had a hell of a defense with Ronnie Lott, Dwight Hicks, Carlton Williamson, Keena Turner and all those guys. Well, in 2011, Patrick Willis, Aldon Smith and Justin Smith just dominated people.

We didn't get to the next level – but we almost did. And it was almost the same kind of change in atmosphere around the

Bay Area. People had given up on the 49ers, thinking they weren't a good team, and Jim Harbaugh came in and changes the whole attitude.

I think it's our time again. It's time for us to come out from the depths and start surfing the top of the water again.

A Breakthrough for Alex Smith

Before Harbaugh arrived, Alex Smith's future looked pretty murky. He'd taken his lumps after the 49ers took him with the No. 1 overall pick in 2005. It didn't help that the 49ers had passed over a local kid named Aaron Rodgers, from Cal, who instead went on to have a dazzling career with the Green Bay Packers.

Alex suffered by comparison. But here's the thing: It wasn't his fault. Alex had impossible circumstances. In his first seven seasons, Alex had seven different offensive coordinators. That's too much to ask of any player, let alone a raw, young quarterback. I guarantee you that if I had that many coordinators I would have struggled, too.

Still, Alex occasionally flashed some potential – he had a solid season with Norv Turner calling plays in 2006 — but it took Harbaugh's special abilities to lift Alex Smith to another level. What Harbaugh did was figure out what Alex did best – and then tailored the offense accordingly. That's that same knack Bill Walsh had, the ability to maximize the talent on his roster by understanding each player's strength.

Harbaugh gave Alex that confidence and told him: "Pull the trigger." That was the key, that confidence. Once Alex had the respect of his teammates, he could show people he was a leader. I love every bit of his attitude.

New Face of Greatness

I'll never forget a conversation I had with linebacker Patrick Willis back in 2008. This was just his second year in the NFL, a time when most players are still trying to find their way, but this kid already had things figured out.

Patrick said to me, "Do you know why I'm playing the game? It's because I want to be in the Hall of Fame some day."

That blew me away. I said, "Wow, you're too young to be talking about that!" In my second year, I was still trying to figure out who I was, just trying to fit in. But Patrick already knows who he is. That resonated with me. I love him. He's amazing.

With every passing year, Patrick gets better and better and his goal of earning enshrinement in Canton looks more attainable. He became the first 49ers player ever to reach the Pro Bowl in each of his first five seasons. Patrick is always ranks among the NFL's league leaders in tackles because he hits hard and because he's fast enough to chase down everything in sight.

And when Willis gets an interception, watch out. He picked off a pass against the Seattle Seahawks in '08 and ran it back 88 yards for a touchdown. You can't tackle him because makes moves better than most running backs.

Patrick Willis is from another planet. He plays at 150 mph. He plays smart. He plays to win. He has a lot of passion. And he knows his history. That's what's going to help his journey as he makes his way toward being a Hall of Famer.

Confidence in Jed York

In the same way that Harbaugh is a clone of Bill Walsh, Jed York reminds me of his uncle, Eddie DeBartolo.

Since taking over as the 49ers' chief executive officer, Jed has done all the right things. More than anything, he finally got us a new stadium. That was huge. Candlestick Park had to go – it was the worst stadium in the NFL. And Jed kept pushing until he got voter approval and then secured the necessary funding for a new stadium in Santa Clara. The 49ers broke ground on a new stadium on April 19, 2012 – and I was thrilled to be there when the first shovel hit the ground.

The new stadium is set to open in 2014 and I made sure my company, Tibco Software, bought a corporate suite for the next 20 years. If you see an old dude with a cane hobbling around the stadium in about 2034, you'll know that's me.

A new home is going to bring a whole new attitude. Players are going to want to create history in a new stadium, and that's the way it should be. The 49ers of today shouldn't be about what our teams built. They shouldn't even be thinking about what we did, those five Super Bowl rings. Let's build on these next five rings. Let's get the next decade going.

Jed understands that. He's doing it his way. He's got this incredible charm when it comes to reaching out to the corporate level, and that's what's going to help the 49ers' brand grow way beyond what it was during my playing days. There are so many more powerful companies in Silicon Valley than there were in the 1980s and Jed is doing a great job of befriending the business community on behalf of the franchise. He brought in Gideon Yu, who was the once the Chief Financial Officer for both Facebook and YouTube, to serve as the 49ers' president and co-owner.

Jed is willing to invest in the right players, too. He's paid his big dogs — Frank Gore, Patrick Willis and Vernon Davis. Then he paid the money to go out and get some good guys in free agency as well. He's definitely a clone of Mr. D.

All the Right Moves

General Manager Trent Baalke, who was promoted to general manager in 2011, understands that putting together a football team goes beyond identifying talent. You have to make sure the pieces fit together. You have to build a sense of chemistry, too.

Bill Walsh recognized that, as so did his right hand man in the front office. John McVay was an executive for all five Super Bowl winning seasons. John did all of the contracts and made sure we had the right players who fit in.

Right now, Trent is the brains behind free agency, the trades and the drafts. He's clearly a smart guy and he Jim Harbaugh see eye-to-eye very well and they're on the same page.

I told Trent, "You guys have the secret sauce and I like how it tastes." He cracked up when I told him that.

Still on the Run

There are lots of troubling stories in the news lately about former NFL players who struggle mentally and physically once their playing days are over. Depression and long-term issues are very serious problems, and I give credit to Commissioner Roger Goodell for making strides in taking better care of retired players.

I've been fortunate. It's helped that it's always been important for me to keep seeking new challenges. Jerry Rice is the same way – he's always on the go. It's like we've never stopped charging up "The Hill" to push ourselves to get ready for the next goal.

Even into my 50s, I'm still piling up big yardage. I've run nine marathons, nine half-marathons and founded the Rock 'n' Roll Half-Marathon in San Jose. I run 40 to 50 miles a week, every week, to stay in shape. If there was a marathon tomorrow, I could run it.

I love the endurance element. Six miles in, I'm just getting started. To get through the finish line, you have to have the right mental attitude: You just have to think about something positive and keep reminding yourself that you've been there before.

Really, training for marathons is no less challenging than the workouts Jerry and I used to put ourselves through every off-season. Whenever newcomers tried to join us, they had no idea what they were getting into. Some rookie would ask 'How many more of these sprints are we going to do?' Oh, that really ticked us off. We'd say, "When we stop running, that's when you stop running."

I stay competitive in the business world, too. Since 1999, I've been the director of business development at Tibco Software, Inc. in Palo Alto. Vivek Ranadive, the CEO, is my new Bill Walsh. He's an innovator and a leader and he inspires me every day.

Better Days Ahead

It was really tough to watch the organization suffer through such a long playoff drought. But you can only stay down in the valley for so long. You find a way to come out and come up back up that hill.

Fans are re-energized. But it's a new set of fans. We're always grateful for the longtime loyalists — they're the Forty-Niner Faithful. But we have a whole new generation now, which is awesome.

We also have the right leader to help us stay on that path. Jim Harbaugh is a winner. He wins wherever he goes. We won't be in that hole as long as he's around. Trust me.

Appendix

CAREER
STATISTICS

ROGER CRAIG

College	Att.	Rushing Yds.	Avg.	TDs	No.	Receiving Yds.	Avg.	TD
1979 Nebraska	7	31	4.4	0	0	0	0	0
1980 Nebraska	108	769	7.1	15	0	0	0	0
1981 Nebraska	173	1060	6.1	6	12	87	7.3	0
1982 Nebraska	119	586	4.9	5	4	15	3.8	0
Career	407	2446	6.0	26	16	102	6.4	0
Professional								
1983 S.F.	176	725	4.1	8	48	427	8.9	4
1984 S.F.	155	649	4.2	7	71	675	9.5	3
1985 S.F.	214	1050	4.9	9	92	1016	11.0	6
1986 S.F.	204	830	4.1	7	81	624	7.7	0
1987 S.F.	215	815	3.8	3	66	492	7.5	1
1988 S.F.	310	1502	4.8	9	76	534	7.0	1
1989 S.F.	271	1054	3.9	6	49	473	9.7	1
1990 S.F.	141	439	3.1	1	25	201	8.0	0
1991 L.A. Raiders	162	590	3.6	1	17	136	8.0	0
1992 Minnesota	105	416	4.0	4	22	164	7.5	0
1993 Minnesota	38	119	3.1	1	19	169	8.9	1
Career	1991	8189	4.1	56	566	4911	8.7	17
Playoffs	207	843	4.1	7	63	606	9.6	2